Self Discipline

How to Use Self Control and Mental Toughness

(Develop Navy Seal Mental Toughness, Unbreakable Grit, Spartan Mindset, Build Good Habits)

Joseph Williams

Published By **Tyson Maxwell**

Joseph Williams

All Rights Reserved

Self Discipline: How to Use Self Control and Mental Toughness (Develop Navy Seal Mental Toughness, Unbreakable Grit, Spartan Mindset, Build Good Habits)

ISBN 978-1-7771996-4-7

No part of this guidebook shall be reproduced in any form without permission in writing from the publisher except in the case of brief quotations embodied in critical articles or reviews.

Legal & Disclaimer

The information contained in this book is not designed to replace or take the place of any form of medicine or professional medical advice. The information in this book has been provided for educational & entertainment purposes only.

The information contained in this book has been compiled from sources deemed reliable, and it is accurate to the best of the Author's knowledge; however, the Author cannot guarantee its accuracy and validity and cannot be held liable for any errors or omissions. Changes are periodically made to this book. You must consult your doctor or get professional medical advice before using any of the suggested remedies, techniques, or information in this book.

Upon using the information contained in this book, you agree to hold harmless the Author from and against any damages, costs, and expenses, including any legal fees potentially resulting from the application of any of the information provided by this guide. This disclaimer applies to any damages or injury caused by the use and application, whether directly or indirectly, of any advice or information presented, whether for breach of contract, tort, negligence, personal injury, criminal intent, or under any other cause of action.

You agree to accept all risks of using the information presented inside this book. You need to consult a professional medical practitioner in order to ensure you are both able and healthy enough to participate in this program.

Table Of Contents

Chapter 1: Explanation Of Self-Discipline . 1

Chapter 2: Definition Of Self-Discipline 9

Chapter 3: Why Self-Discipline Is Challenging 16

Chapter 4: Improved Productivity 23

Chapter 5: Improved Mental And Emotional Health 29

Chapter 6: Time Management Techniques 39

Chapter 7: Maintaining Motivation 49

Chapter 8: Health And Fitness 61

Chapter 9: Advice 67

Chapter 10: Understanding The Role Of The Mind In Self-Discipline 80

Chapter 11: Setting Clear, Realistic Goals For Motivation And Focus 87

Chapter 12: Overcoming Procrastination And Building Good Habits 93

Chapter 13: The Power Of Positive Thinking And Self-Discipline 99

Chapter 14: How To Overcome Setbacks And Obstacles To Stay Committed To Our Goals 110

Chapter 15: Building Self-Discipline With Self-Awareness And Mindfulness 122

Chapter 16: Exercise And Self-Discipline 128

Chapter 17: The Power Of Accountability In Achieving Goals 135

Chapter 18: The Importance Of Rest And Self-Care In Maintaining Self-Discipline 142

Chapter 19: Fundamental Principles Of Self-Discipline 146

Chapter 20: Physical Excellence Leads To Mastery In Life 159

Chapter 1: Explanation Of Self-Discipline

Self-location is the capability to manipulate one's mind, feelings, and behaviors that allows you to gain a specific purpose. It is the exercise of restraining one's impulses and dreams on the way to attention on what's crucial and essential. Self-hassle is frequently related to power of will, willpower, and self-regulation, and it's far considered an important excellent for reaching fulfillment in all regions of lifestyles.

Self-subject is a discovered behavior that can be superior via conscious effort and workout. It entails making aware alternatives and taking planned movements to align one's actions and behaviors with one's lengthy-term desires and values. Self-subject calls for a excessive diploma of self-awareness and the potential to recognize and manipulate one's personal mind and feelings.

One of the important element factors of strength of thoughts isn't always on time gratification. This approach resisting the urge for fast pride or delight in choice of an prolonged-term reward. For instance, someone who is making an attempt to shed kilos may additionally pick out out to stand up to the temptation of consuming a dessert an awesome way to gain their weight loss desires. A student who is making an attempt to improve their grades may additionally select out to spend their unfastened time reading in desire to looking tv.

Self-place isn't always about being strict or inflexible, but as a substitute approximately making intentional picks that align with one's values and dreams. It is about developing a healthy balance among quick-time period pride and lengthy-time period achievement. Self-subject is not pretty much maintaining off horrible behaviors or conduct, but moreover approximately cultivating exceptional ones. For example, a person who is trying to improve their health may make the deliberate choice to exercising frequently and eat a balanced weight-reduction plan.

Self-vicinity is also intently related to motivation. In order to be self-disciplined, a person must be precipitated to collect their desires. Motivation offers the energy and electricity wished to overcome obstacles and persevere thru tough instances. Self-concern, but, gives the form and framework wished to expose motivation into motion.

Finally, electricity of will is a non-forestall method that requires ongoing attempt and determination. It isn't something that may be achieved in a single day or thru a unmarried act of self-discipline. It requires exercising and staying energy if you want to expand the behavior and behaviors that purpose lengthy-term success.

In give up, energy of will is the capability to control one's thoughts, emotions, and behaviors in case you want to attain a selected aim. It includes making deliberate options that align with one's values and dreams, and requires a excessive degree of self-popularity and motivation. Self-problem isn't always approximately being inflexible or strict, but alternatively approximately developing a healthful stability amongst short-term pride and prolonged-time period success. It is a found out conduct that calls for ongoing exercising and dedication, and is vital for accomplishing success in all regions of lifestyles.

Importance of Self-Discipline in Achieving Success

Self-place is a crucial trouble in accomplishing fulfillment in all regions of life. Whether it's far in non-public relationships, academic pursuits, or expert endeavors, strength of will is an important excellent that permits people to triumph over limitations and gain their dreams.

One of the primary blessings of self-discipline is that it permits people to preserve recognition and avoid distractions. With the abundance of distractions in modern-day-day international, it is simple to turn out to be sidetracked through things that do not make a contribution to at least one's dreams. However, with energy of thoughts, people are capable of stay on the right track and consciousness on the matters that rely.

Self-vicinity is also essential for growing well conduct and breaking lousy ones. Habits are powerful drivers of conduct, and people who lack power of mind frequently locate themselves stuck in terrible sorts of conduct. However, with electricity of will, people are able to expand first-rate conduct that make contributions to their fulfillment, at the equal time as moreover breaking lousy behavior that preserve them once more.

In addition, power of will is important for handling time effectively. Successful people apprehend that thing is a restrained useful resource, and that they need to apply it correctly so one can acquire their dreams. With strength of will, humans are capable of prioritize their duties, keep away from procrastination, and control their time efficiently.

Self-problem is also vital for maintaining motivation and perseverance. Success isn't often carried out with out setbacks and traumatic conditions, and people who lack self-control regularly give up at the same time as faced with problems. However, with self-control, humans are capable of keep motivation and push through limitations a good way to reap their goals.

Finally, strength of will is essential for growing a strong work ethic. Success often calls for difficult paintings and backbone, and those who lack willpower often war to region within the critical try. However, with strength of will, people are capable of boom a sturdy artwork ethic that allows them to acquire their desires through consistent attempt and staying strength.

In give up, strength of mind is an important incredible for accomplishing success in all areas of lifestyles. It lets in people to keep focus and avoid distractions, increase appropriate conduct and wreck terrible ones, manipulate time efficaciously, preserve motivation and perseverance, and broaden a sturdy art work ethic. Without electricity of will, humans are possibly to conflict of their hobbies and might fail to attain their goals. However, with power of mind, human beings are in a role to triumph over limitations and accumulate their entire capability.

This e-book, titled "Mastering the Art of Self-Discipline: The Key to Achieving Success in Life," is a complete manual to understanding and developing power of thoughts as a device for achieving fulfillment in all areas of lifestyles.

The ebook is cut up into severa chapters, every of which focuses on a distinct factor of strength of mind. Chapter 2, "Explanation of Self-Discipline," gives an in-depth definition of self-control and explores its significance in project success. Chapter three, "Importance of Self-Discipline in Achieving Success," delves into the advantages of self-control and why it is this kind of vital issue in achieving fulfillment.

Chapter 4, "Building Self-Discipline," offers sensible techniques for growing energy of mind, which incorporates placing dreams and priorities, breaking lousy conduct, time control strategies, and techniques to overcome procrastination. Chapter five, "Staying Disciplined," specializes in preserving strength of mind over the long term, collectively with hints for staying brought about, steady, and overcoming setbacks.

Chapter 2: Definition Of Self-Discipline

Self-place is the potential to manipulate one's mind, feelings, and behaviors in case you need to gain a particular aim. It consists of making conscious options and taking planned moves to align one's movements and behaviors with one's prolonged-time period desires and values. In essence, self-discipline is the exercise of restraining one's impulses and desires an tremendous manner to reputation on what is essential and crucial.

Self-subject is a located out conduct that may be evolved through aware try and practice. It calls for a immoderate degree of self-interest and the capacity to understand and control one's private thoughts and feelings. Self-area is often related to strength of thoughts, willpower, and self-regulation, and it's miles taken into consideration an important superb for engaging in fulfillment in all areas of existence.

One of the important element additives of self-discipline isn't always on time gratification. This technique resisting the urge for instant satisfaction or pleasure in opt for of an extended-time period praise. For instance, someone who is attempting to shed pounds might also pick out out to withstand the temptation of consuming a dessert that allows you to acquire their weight reduction goals. A scholar who is trying to enhance their grades may pick out out to spend their unfastened time studying in place of watching television.

Self-subject is not about being inflexible or overly strict, but as an opportunity about making intentional options that align with one's values and dreams. It is about developing a healthful stability among quick-time period delight and extended-term fulfillment. Self-area isn't pretty an lousy lot averting bad behaviors or conduct, but moreover approximately cultivating excessive extremely good ones. For instance, a person who is trying to enhance their health may also furthermore make the deliberate preference to exercising often and devour a balanced food regimen.

Self-area is closely associated with motivation. In order to be self-disciplined, a person need to be inspired to acquire their goals. Motivation presents the strain and power desired to conquer obstacles and persevere through hard instances. Self-discipline, but, offers the form and framework preferred to show motivation into motion.

In cease, electricity of will is the functionality to control one's mind, feelings, and behaviors so that you can acquire a selected motive. It consists of making aware picks and taking deliberate movements to align one's movements and behaviors with one's lengthy-time period goals and values. Self-place is a discovered conduct that can be advanced through aware attempt and exercise, and it's far considered an crucial great for accomplishing achievement in all regions of life. By growing strength of will, human beings are capable of face up to immediate gratification, make intentional picks, and live targeted on their prolonged-term desires.

Myths and Misconceptions About Self-Discipline

Self-project is an critical remarkable that allows humans to advantage their dreams and acquire their whole capability. However, there are various myths and misconceptions approximately electricity of mind that may prevent human beings from growing this important skills. In this bankruptcy, we're capable of explore a number of the most commonplace myths and misconceptions approximately electricity of will.

Myth 1: Self-location is innate and can not be decided.

One of the most commonplace myths about strength of will is that it is an innate high-quality that a few people are born with and others aren't. This is really now not genuine. While some people can also have a natural inclination closer to strength of thoughts, it is a competencies that may be learned and developed thru exercising.

Myth 2: Self-concern is ready depriving oneself of satisfaction.

Another common misconception about self-discipline is that it's far all about denying oneself of delight and dwelling a life of austerity. In fact, power of thoughts is prepared locating a wholesome stability among short-time period satisfaction and lengthy-term achievement. It is not about denying oneself of pride altogether, but as an alternative about making intentional options that align with one's values and desires.

Myth 3: Self-area is only favored for unsightly duties.

Many human beings keep in mind that strength of thoughts is best essential for completing ugly or dull obligations. However, electricity of will is also vital for achieving goals which is probably exciting and exciting. For example, a musician may additionally furthermore want energy of thoughts to exercise their tool for hours each day, or an athlete may moreover need self-control to hold a rigorous schooling regimen.

Myth four: Self-assignment is about being inflexible and inflexible.

Some human beings trust that strength of mind requires being rigid and inflexible in a unmarried's technique to life. However, power of will is not about being overly strict or rigid. It is set making intentional alternatives that align with one's values and dreams even as moreover taking into account flexibility and edition.

Myth 5: Self-challenge is just like strength of will.

While strength of mind and willpower are carefully related, they are now not the same trouble. Willpower is the functionality to face up to on the spot temptations and make selections that align with lengthy-term dreams. Self-region, as an alternative, is the exercising of continuously making intentional selections that align with one's values and dreams.

In end, there are numerous myths and misconceptions approximately willpower that may save you people from growing this vital knowledge. Self-location isn't always an innate excellent that cannot be discovered, nor is it about depriving oneself of pleasure or being rigid and inflexible. Instead, power of thoughts is a determined out behavior that can be developed thru practice, and it's far approximately locating a healthy stability among brief-term delight and long-time period success. By dispelling those myths and misconceptions, people can better apprehend the actual nature of energy of will and paintings closer to developing this critical talents.

Chapter 3: Why Self-Discipline Is Challenging

While electricity of will is an crucial terrific for attaining achievement in all areas of lifestyles, it is not continually smooth to develop and preserve. There are numerous traumatic conditions that individuals may additionally additionally additionally face whilst trying to develop electricity of will, and understanding the ones stressful situations is an crucial step in overcoming them. In this financial break, we can discover some of the number one reasons why energy of will is tough.

Challenge 1: Overcoming right away gratification

One of the maximum essential annoying conditions of power of mind is overcoming the temptation of without delay gratification. It is human nature to are looking for satisfaction and keep away from pain, and as a forestall end result, we regularly prioritize quick-time period pride over extended-time period goals. For instance, someone can also choose to look at television in choice to analyzing for an exam as it presents immediately pride. Overcoming this temptation calls for a immoderate degree of self-reputation and the capability to remove gratification in desire of prolonged-term rewards.

Challenge 2: Breaking awful behavior

Habits are powerful drivers of conduct, and breaking terrible behavior is one in every of the biggest disturbing situations of self-discipline. Habits are deeply ingrained in our brains and can be tough to trade. For instance, someone can also additionally moreover warfare to surrender smoking or overeating due to the reality those conduct have end up deeply ingrained of their every day normal. Breaking the ones behavior calls for a conscious try and the improvement of latest, brilliant behavior.

Challenge three: Dealing with distractions

In current global, there are countless distractions that would derail even the maximum disciplined people. Social media, email, and different virtual distractions can results thieve our hobby and save you us from focusing on our prolonged-term desires. Dealing with distractions requires a sturdy revel in of electricity of will and the functionality to stay focused on what is critical.

Challenge four: Managing strain and emotions

Stress and feelings can also gift a exquisite challenge to strength of mind. When we're harassed or emotional, we're more likely to make impulsive picks that aren't aligned with our lengthy-term dreams. Additionally, pressure can motive us to lose consciousness and end up distracted, making it hard to keep strength of will. Managing pressure and emotions calls for the development of coping strategies that permit us to stay targeted and centered even inside the face of disturbing situations.

Challenge five: Consistency and staying energy

Finally, retaining power of mind over the long term requires consistency and endurance. It is simple to be disciplined for a fast period of time, however maintaining electricity of will over the long time calls for ongoing attempt and determination. It can be tough to live inspired and maintain consciousness, particularly at the same time as confronted with setbacks and worrying situations.

In quit, self-control is a tough understanding to broaden and maintain. Overcoming on the spot gratification, breaking awful conduct, dealing with distractions, dealing with strain and feelings, and keeping consistency and persistence are a number of the largest worrying situations of strength of thoughts. However, with the useful resource of records those worrying conditions and developing strategies to conquer them, people can boom self-discipline and acquire success in all areas of life.

Achieving Goals and Success

Self-place is a crucial thing in attaining achievement and engaging in a single's dreams. By growing strength of will, human beings are capable of make intentional choices that align with their prolonged-time period dreams and values, and keep away from distractions and temptations which could prevent them from attaining their entire ability. In this financial catastrophe, we're capable of find out how strength of will can assist humans attain their dreams and collect fulfillment in all areas of existence.

Setting Goals

The first step in reaching achievement is placing easy and measurable dreams. By setting particular and conceivable goals, human beings can create a roadmap for achievement and tune their development alongside the way. Setting desires moreover offers motivation and cognizance, giving humans a smooth experience of purpose and path.

Breaking Bad Habits

One of the maximum essential elements of strength of mind is breaking horrible behavior which may be keeping human beings decrease once more. Bad conduct can be a major impediment to achievement, and they will be capable of save you human beings from conducting their entire potential. By developing power of thoughts, people can smash those conduct and update them with quality behaviors that beneficial useful resource their extended-term desires.

Managing Time Effectively

Time manipulate is a important potential for carrying out fulfillment. With electricity of thoughts, human beings are able to prioritize their responsibilities and keep away from procrastination, making the most in their time and maximizing their productiveness. Effective time control allows individuals to reap more in masses much less time, releasing up time for one-of-a-kind essential sports activities activities and pursuits.

Maintaining Motivation and Perseverance

Success isn't regularly carried out without setbacks and demanding situations. With electricity of will, humans are capable of hold motivation and perseverance in the face of adversity. Self-region presents the form and framework needed to live focused on prolonged-time period dreams, despite the fact that confronted with obstacles and setbacks.

Developing a Strong Work Ethic

Success regularly calls for tough paintings and strength of mind. With electricity of will, people are able to enlarge a robust paintings ethic that permits them to accumulate their goals via regular attempt and staying electricity. A sturdy paintings ethic is a key issue in attaining fulfillment in all regions of lifestyles, from non-public relationships to professional endeavors.

Chapter 4: Improved Productivity

Self-place is a critical factor in improving productiveness. By developing power of thoughts, individuals are able to interest their strength and efforts on what is most important, warding off distractions and time-dropping sports that can reduce productivity. In this chapter, we will explore how strength of will can assist humans enhance their productivity and gather extra in a lot much less time.

Avoiding Procrastination

Procrastination is sincerely one of the most crucial obstacles to productiveness. When people procrastinate, they waste valuable time and power that is probably better spent on more essential sports activities. With energy of will, humans are able to avoid procrastination and live focused on their goals, making the most of their time and maximizing their productivity.

Setting Priorities

Effective productivity calls for putting smooth priorities and focusing on what's most important. With self-control, humans are capable of turn out to be privy to their pinnacle priorities and allocate their time and power as a cease result. This permits them to keep away from distractions and time-losing sports activities, making the maximum in their time and maximizing their productiveness.

Managing Time Effectively

Time manipulate is a important issue in productivity. With strength of will, human beings are able to control their time effectively, prioritizing their obligations and averting time-dropping sports. Effective time manage permits humans to obtain extra in plenty less time, developing productivity and releasing up time for different important sports.

Creating Positive Habits

Self-vicinity is crucial for growing first-class behavior that useful resource productiveness.

By growing electricity of will, human beings are able to create exquisite behavior, collectively with everyday exercising or meditation, that help their regular properly-being and enhance their productivity. These behavior provide a shape and recurring that makes it less complicated to live targeted and powerful.

Staying Focused

Staying centered is important for productiveness. With strength of mind, human beings are capable of stay targeted on their goals, avoiding distractions and one in every of a kind activities which could lessen their productivity. Staying centered calls for a immoderate degree of self-attention and the ability to control one's mind and feelings, which may be superior through strength of will.

In conclusion, strength of will is a essential detail in improving productivity. By avoiding procrastination, setting priorities, managing time efficiently, growing extremely good conduct, and staying centered, people are able to advantage greater in much less time, developing their productiveness and accomplishing their desires. Through energy of will, people are able to make intentional options that align with their values and goals, and keep away from distractions and time-dropping activities that may reduce productivity. By developing strength of will, human beings can release their entire potential and gain success in all areas of existence.

Better Decision-Making

Self-vicinity is an crucial best for making better decisions. By growing electricity of will, humans are capable of control their mind and feelings, make deliberate alternatives, and align their actions with their prolonged-term dreams and values. In this monetary catastrophe, we're capable of find out how electricity of will can assist human beings make higher options and accumulate success in all areas of life.

Developing Self-Awareness

Self-recognition is a crucial detail in making higher selections. With self-discipline, humans are capable of amplify self-popularity, knowledge their mind and emotions, and the way they have an effect on their choice-making. This lets in them to make more planned options, thinking about the potential outcomes in their actions in advance than you make a decision.

Avoiding Impulsive Decisions

Impulsive selections may be unfavorable to reaching fulfillment. With power of mind, humans are capable of keep away from impulsive selections, taking the time to endure in thoughts their alternatives and make deliberate options which might be consistent with their lengthy-term dreams and values. This permits them to avoid the capability lousy results of impulsive choices and make extra thoughtful alternatives.

Reducing Stress and Anxiety

Stress and tension may have a massive impact on choice-making. With energy of will, people are able to manage strain and tension, maintaining a clean and centered attitude that facilitates better selection-making. This allows them to make more thoughtful and planned alternatives, even in the face of disturbing situations and setbacks.

Developing a Long-Term Perspective

Self-scenario permits human beings to expand a protracted-term mind-set, considering the capability outcomes in their alternatives over the prolonged-term. This permits them to make alternatives that align with their lengthy-term dreams and values, although it requires brief-term sacrifices or hard options.

Chapter 5: Improved Mental And Emotional Health

Self-region isn't handiest vital for challenge fulfillment, however it's also important for reinforcing intellectual and emotional fitness. By growing self-control, people are able to manage their thoughts and emotions, hold a amazing outlook, and domesticate a healthy and balanced lifestyle. In this financial catastrophe, we're capable of discover how strength of thoughts can improve intellectual and emotional fitness and well-being.

Reducing Stress and Anxiety

Stress and anxiety may have a super effect on highbrow and emotional fitness. With strength of will, people are able to manage pressure and anxiety, maintaining a easy and targeted mind-set that permits better decision-making and promotes conventional well-being. This permits humans to hold a pleasant outlook and reduce the terrible effects of stress and tension.

Developing Self-Awareness

Self-cognizance is a crucial element in improving highbrow and emotional health. With power of thoughts, human beings are capable of growth self-consciousness, expertise their thoughts and emotions, and the way they've got an effect on their intellectual and emotional fitness. This lets in them to grow to be aware about capacity assets of strain and tension and increase techniques to manipulate them efficiently.

Creating Positive Habits

Self-problem is crucial for growing super behavior that guide intellectual and emotional health. By growing electricity of will, human beings can set up brilliant behavior which includes ordinary exercising, healthful eating, and meditation that manual their commonplace nicely-being and reduce strain and tension. These conduct provide a structure and regular that promotes stability and nicely-being.

Maintaining a Positive Outlook

Maintaining a exquisite outlook is critical for highbrow and emotional fitness. With energy of thoughts, human beings are capable of preserve a awesome outlook, specializing in what's internal their control and warding off horrible self-communicate and rumination. This allows them to maintain a healthful and balanced mind-set that enables their regular properly-being.

Developing Resilience

Resilience is an crucial hassle in intellectual and emotional fitness. With energy of will, individuals are able to expand resilience, the capacity to get higher from setbacks and disturbing situations. This permits individuals to keep a pleasing outlook, even inside the face of adversity, and extend techniques to address strain and tension successfully.

In forestall, strength of will is an essential splendid for enhancing intellectual and emotional fitness. By lowering strain and anxiety, developing self-recognition, developing great habits, preserving a nice outlook, and developing resilience, people are able to promote normal nicely-being and gain success in all areas of lifestyles. Through self-control, people can cultivate a healthy and balanced life-style that helps their intellectual and emotional fitness and properly-being.

Setting Goals and Priorities

Self-situation is an essential wonderful for placing and achieving dreams. By growing willpower, people are capable of set smooth and possible dreams, prioritize their tasks, and work toward their extended-term dreams. In this financial disaster, we're able to discover how energy of thoughts can help people set desires and priorities and benefit fulfillment in all regions of life.

Setting Clear and Measurable Goals

The first step in undertaking success is placing clean and measurable dreams. With self-discipline, people are able to set specific and feasible desires, developing a roadmap for achievement and monitoring their development along the way. Setting goals additionally gives motivation and awareness, giving human beings a easy revel in of purpose and route.

Breaking Down Goals into Smaller Tasks

Breaking down dreams into smaller obligations is critical for undertaking achievement. With self-discipline, individuals are capable to break down large goals into smaller, more practicable responsibilities, making it lots much less hard to live endorsed and focused. This additionally allows people to track their development and modify their approach as desired.

Prioritizing Tasks

Effective time control calls for placing priorities and focusing on what's maximum important. With electricity of thoughts, individuals are able to prioritize their duties, allocating their time and strength to the sports that are maximum crucial. This permits them to keep away from distractions and time-losing sports, making the maximum in their time and maximizing their productiveness.

Staying Focused

Staying targeted is crucial for engaging in success. With willpower, humans are able to stay targeted on their dreams, heading off distractions and different sports activities that might reduce their productiveness. Staying targeted calls for a excessive level of self-interest and the capability to manipulate one's mind and feelings, which can be developed through strength of will.

Adjusting Goals as Needed

Adjusting desires as needed is an important part of the goal-placing method. With self-control, individuals are able to regulate their dreams and strategies as desired, making it less hard to stay encouraged and centered. This allows humans to adapt to converting instances and disturbing situations, making the maximum of their sources and maximizing their possibilities of fulfillment.

In cease, power of will is an vital exquisite for putting dreams and priorities. By placing smooth and measurable dreams, breaking down dreams into smaller obligations, prioritizing responsibilities, staying focused, and adjusting goals as desired, human beings are able to collect success in all areas of life. Through strength of thoughts, people are able to make intentional choices that align with their values and desires, and art work within the course of their prolonged-time period goals with consciousness and backbone.

Breaking Bad Habits and Forming Good Habits

Self-difficulty is crucial for breaking bad conduct and forming well behavior. By growing electricity of mind, people are in a function to triumph over horrific kinds of behavior and set up amazing conduct that beneficial resource their lengthy-term dreams and well-being. In this economic smash, we can discover how strength of mind can assist human beings destroy terrible habits and shape fantastic behavior to gain success in all areas of existence.

Identifying Bad Habits

The first step in breaking horrible conduct is identifying them. With strength of will, human beings are able to boom self-recognition, spotting terrible sorts of behavior which can be retaining them over again. This lets in them to achieve this to interrupt those behavior and update them with tremendous behaviors that manual their prolonged-time period dreams and nicely-being.

Creating a Plan of Action

Creating a course of action is essential for breaking bad behavior and forming specific behavior. With electricity of mind, human beings are capable of expand a plan for breaking terrible behavior and forming new, powerful behavior. This plan have to embody unique steps that individuals can take to conquer horrible behaviors and set up powerful behavior.

Developing Self-Control

Self-manipulate is essential for breaking awful behavior and forming authentic behavior. With energy of mind, humans are capable of increase power of mind, the capability to face as a whole lot as temptation and manage their thoughts and behaviors. This permits them to overcome bad sorts of behavior and set up high-quality behavior that assist their lengthy-time period desires and properly-being.

Replacing Bad Habits with Good Habits

Replacing awful behavior with well behavior is essential for carrying out achievement. With energy of mind, humans are able to replace awful kinds of conduct with super behavior that assist their lengthy-time period dreams and properly-being. This calls for consistent strive and endurance, further to a willingness to make adjustments and take action to obtain one's desires.

Staying Motivated

Staying stimulated is important for breaking horrible behavior and forming relevant habits. With power of mind, people are able to hold motivation and focus, even inside the face of setbacks and annoying conditions. This requires a immoderate degree of self-interest and the capability to govern one's mind and feelings, which can be evolved thru strength of will.

Chapter 6: Time Management Techniques

Self-vicinity is important for effective time management. By developing strength of mind, humans are able to prioritize their responsibilities, avoid distractions, and make the maximum of their time. In this financial disaster, we are able to find out some time manipulate strategies that might help human beings increase their productiveness and acquire their desires.

Pareto Principle

The Pareto principle, also known as the eighty/20 rule, states that 80% of the effects come from 20% of the efforts. This way that human beings need to recognition their time and power at the sports that generate the most tremendous outcomes. By prioritizing their obligations and focusing at the maximum essential sports activities, human beings could make the most of their time and maximize their productiveness.

To-Do Lists

To-do lists are a well-known time control device that can assist human beings stay organized and targeted. By developing a listing of obligations to be completed every day, humans can prioritize their sports activities and make sure that they may be making improvement closer to their desires. To-do lists may be created using masses of device, together with a paper planner, a virtual app, or a whiteboard.

Time Blocking

Time blocking off is a time control method that involves scheduling precise blocks of time for each hobby. This permits humans to prioritize their duties and avoid distractions, making the maximum in their time and growing their productivity. Time blocking can be finished the usage of quite a few device, together with a paper planner or a digital calendar app.

Batching

Batching is a time management technique that entails grouping similar responsibilities collectively and finishing them in a single batch. This can help people keep time and avoid distractions, making the maximum in their time and maximizing their productivity. Batching may be completed to quite a few sports activities, collectively with responding to emails or finishing office paintings.

Avoiding Multitasking

Multitasking may be unfavorable to productiveness. With willpower, people are able to keep away from multitasking, focusing their strength and efforts on one task at a time. This lets in them to make the most in their time and maximize their productivity, keeping off distractions and time-wasting activities.

In prevent, time control is essential for attaining fulfillment. By the usage of time management strategies along side the Pareto principle, to-do lists, time blocking, batching, and averting multitasking, individuals can make the most of their time and benefit their dreams. Through willpower, people can prioritize their responsibilities, keep away from distractions, and reputation their power and efforts on what's maximum essential. By developing energy of mind, humans can unencumber their complete capability and gain fulfillment in all regions of lifestyles.

Strategies to Overcome Procrastination

Procrastination is a common venture that many people face on the same time as trying to gather their goals. With self-control, individuals can boom techniques to conquer procrastination and boom their productiveness. In this bankruptcy, we are able to find out some techniques to conquer procrastination and reap achievement.

Identifying the Root Cause

The first step in overcoming procrastination is figuring out the foundation reason. Procrastination can be as a result of a choice of things, which include worry of failure, loss of motivation, or feeling crushed. By understanding the foundation purpose of procrastination, human beings can boom techniques to triumph over it and take movement to gain their desires.

Breaking Tasks into Smaller Steps

Breaking duties into smaller steps can assist human beings conquer procrastination. With energy of will, human beings can spoil larger obligations into smaller, greater workable steps, making it less complex to get started out and keep away from feeling crushed. This additionally allows humans to track their improvement and keep motivation, making it much less hard to triumph over procrastination and gain their desires.

Creating a Plan of Action

Creating a plan of action is critical for overcoming procrastination. With electricity of will, human beings can create a plan for completing their obligations, setting precise final dates and milestones. This provides a smooth roadmap for reaching their goals and permits human beings live recommended and heading within the right course.

Eliminating Distractions

Eliminating distractions is critical for overcoming procrastination. With strength of will, individuals can grow to be privy to and put off distractions which might be retaining them lower lower back, such as social media, email, or specific time-dropping sports. This lets in them to popularity their power and efforts on their obligations, developing their productivity and helping them conquer procrastination.

Rewarding Progress

Rewarding progress is an powerful approach for overcoming procrastination. With willpower, humans can reward themselves for making improvement inside the direction of their desires, supplying motivation and helping to hold momentum. Rewards can be as simple as taking a wreck or treating oneself to a small indulgence.

In end, procrastination may be a huge impediment to undertaking achievement. By figuring out the foundation purpose of procrastination, breaking duties into smaller steps, developing a direction of motion, putting off distractions, and profitable development, humans can overcome procrastination and growth their productiveness. Through energy of will, people can enlarge the talents and techniques desired to overcome procrastination and gain their dreams, unlocking their complete functionality and accomplishing achievement in all areas of life.

Importance of Consistency

Consistency is an critical detail of achievement. With power of will, people can growth consistent conduct and behaviors that resource their long-term desires and properly-being. In this economic ruin, we can discover the importance of consistency and the manner strength of thoughts can help human beings attain success via consistency.

Establishing Trust and Credibility

Consistency is vital for establishing consider and credibility. With electricity of will, human beings can installation ordinary habits and behaviors, that could assist them assemble a reputation for reliability and trustworthiness. This is vital for achievement in hundreds of areas of lifestyles, collectively with commercial enterprise, relationships, and private development.

Creating Momentum

Consistency creates momentum. With energy of mind, humans can establish constant conduct and behaviors that help their long-time period dreams and properly-being. This creates a revel in of momentum and development, which may be a effective motivator for accomplishing success. This momentum can help people live heading within the proper route and make development closer to their desires, even inside the face of setbacks and traumatic conditions.

Developing Mastery

Consistency is essential for growing mastery. With willpower, people can installation everyday behavior and behaviors that permit them to expand mastery of their situation or region of hobby. This calls for regular strive and workout, as well as a willingness to take a look at and enhance through the years. Through consistency, people can extend the abilities and know-how needed to achieve fulfillment and make a effective effect of their area.

Building Resilience

Consistency is critical for constructing resilience. With strength of mind, humans can set up regular conduct and behaviors that assist their extended-time period dreams and well-being. This calls for a excessive diploma of self-awareness and the capacity to govern one's thoughts and feelings, which may be advanced via power of mind. By constructing resilience, humans can conquer setbacks and traumatic conditions, and preserve to make improvement inside the direction of their desires.

Creating a Strong Foundation

Consistency creates a strong basis for achievement. With self-discipline, humans can set up steady behavior and behaviors that resource their lengthy-time period desires and well-being. This creates a sturdy basis for achievement, offering a framework for engaging in one's dreams and growing a top notch impact within the global.

Chapter 7: Maintaining Motivation

Motivation is vital for accomplishing fulfillment. With electricity of thoughts, humans can boom the talents and strategies needed to hold motivation, even in the face of setbacks and challenges. In this chapter, we can discover how self-discipline can help individuals keep motivation and advantage fulfillment.

Setting Goals

Setting dreams is essential for preserving motivation. With strength of mind, people can set particular, measurable, doable, relevant, and time-certain (SMART) goals that provide a smooth roadmap for reaching fulfillment. These desires may be damaged down into smaller, more viable steps, making it less complicated to stay encouraged and centered.

Creating a Vision

Creating a imaginative and prescient is vital for retaining motivation. With strength of thoughts, human beings can create a imaginative and prescient for his or her future, visualizing the shape of life they want to stay and the type of man or woman they want to turn out to be. This imaginative and prescient can function a powerful motivator, providing the foundation and stress had to reap one's goals.

Tracking Progress

Tracking development is crucial for retaining motivation. With energy of thoughts, people can music their development inside the course of their goals, using device alongside aspect a magazine, a spreadsheet, or a addiction-monitoring app. This allows individuals to appearance the development they may be making, which may be a effective motivator for continuing to make development.

Celebrating Achievements

Celebrating achievements is essential for retaining motivation. With power of mind, people may have fun their achievements, irrespective of how small, providing a feel of success and delight. This can help people live prompted and inspired, even in the face of setbacks and worrying situations.

Staying Positive

Staying awesome is important for preserving motivation. With electricity of will, human beings can cultivate a first rate mind-set, focusing at the possibilities and capacity benefits of setbacks and disturbing situations. This requires the ability to control one's mind and feelings, which can be developed through electricity of mind.

In conclusion, preserving motivation is important for accomplishing success. By putting dreams, growing a vision, monitoring development, celebrating achievements, and staying powerful, people can hold motivation and acquire their desires. Through strength of will, humans can extend the competencies and techniques had to live added approximately and targeted, even within the face of setbacks and challenges. By prioritizing self-control, people can acquire success in all areas of life, unlocking their entire potential and growing a powerful effect inside the global.

Creating a Support System

Creating a help device is vital for mission fulfillment. With power of thoughts, people can make bigger the skills and strategies needed to assemble a community of help, that could offer steering, encouragement, and motivation. In this chapter, we're able to discover how power of will can assist individuals create a assist device and gain fulfillment.

Identifying Needs

The first step in developing a useful useful resource device is identifying one's needs. With strength of will, humans can have a look at their strengths and weaknesses, similarly to their desires and aspirations. This can assist them find out the types of help they need, together with mentorship, accountability, or emotional aid.

Building a Network

Building a community of useful resource is vital for venture fulfillment. With power of will, humans can accumulate out to friends, circle of relatives, or expert networks, building relationships that could offer steering, encouragement, and motivation. This network also can offer get right of access to to new opportunities, assets, and facts, that may help people obtain their goals.

Seeking Professional Help

Seeking expert assistance is essential for developing a help machine. With energy of thoughts, people can are looking for help from professionals, which includes coaches, therapists, or mentors. These experts can provide specialized understanding and steering, helping human beings collect their dreams and overcome obstacles.

Joining Groups and Communities

Joining groups and groups is important for developing a resource tool. With energy of mind, people can be part of agencies and corporations that percentage their hobbies and dreams, building relationships with like-minded human beings. This can offer a enjoy of network and belonging, further to possibilities for collaboration and getting to know.

Offering Support to Others

Offering guide to others is essential for growing a help tool. With self-discipline, people can offer help to others, building relationships based totally on mutual aid and encouragement. This can offer a experience of motive and achievement, in addition to opportunities for private growth and studying.

In surrender, developing a assist machine is critical for attaining success. By figuring out desires, building a network, seeking out expert assist, becoming a member of companies and groups, and imparting resource to others, human beings can create a community of guide which can offer steerage, encouragement, and motivation. Through power of will, people can broaden the capabilities and strategies had to bring together and keep a support device, unlocking their complete functionality and undertaking success in all regions of life.

Career and Work

Career and paintings are essential factors of 1's lifestyles, and power of will plays a important function in reaching fulfillment in the ones areas. In this financial disaster, we're capable of discover how self-control can help human beings gain success in their profession and art work.

Developing a Clear Vision

Developing a easy imaginative and prescient is important for reaching fulfillment in a unmarried's profession and paintings. With strength of will, people can outline their long-time period career dreams and create a course of action for engaging in them. This calls for a excessive stage of self-cognizance and the ability to govern one's thoughts and feelings, which may be evolved through strength of mind.

Building and Maintaining Skills

Building and retaining skills is important for reaching fulfillment in a single's career and artwork. With strength of mind, humans can make investments time and energy in studying new capabilities and enhancing present ones. This calls for a commitment to lifelong studying and a willingness to take on new traumatic situations and possibilities.

Managing Time and Priorities

Managing time and priorities is crucial for assignment fulfillment in a unmarried's profession and artwork. With self-discipline, human beings can prioritize their responsibilities and control their time correctly, making the most of their workday. This requires the capacity to keep away from distractions and hold awareness at the most crucial duties.

Networking and Building Relationships

Networking and building relationships is vital for reaching fulfillment in a unmarried's profession and artwork. With willpower, people can make investments time and power in building relationships with colleagues, mentors, and exceptional experts. This requires a commitment to constructing considerable relationships and offering fee to others.

Taking Risks and Seizing Opportunities

Taking dangers and seizing opportunities is vital for conducting fulfillment in one's career and art work. With power of mind, human beings can growth the braveness and self notion needed to tackle new traumatic conditions and seize possibilities. This requires a willingness to step outside of one's consolation place and embody uncertainty.

In quit, power of mind performs a vital feature in reaching achievement in a unmarried's career and paintings. By developing a clean vision, constructing and preserving capabilities, dealing with time and priorities, networking and constructing relationships, and taking risks and seizing possibilities, human beings can attain achievement and make a top notch effect in their area. Through strength of will, human beings can amplify the abilities and strategies needed to collect achievement in all areas of lifestyles, unlocking their entire ability and developing a high splendid impact within the international.

Personal Finances

Personal price range are an important difficulty of one's life, and strength of will plays a vital characteristic in attaining economic success. In this economic catastrophe, we're capable of discover how strength of mind can assist people achieve monetary success.

Developing a Budget

Developing a rate variety is vital for reaching economic fulfillment. With self-discipline, people can create a rate variety that aligns with their financial dreams and priorities, offering a smooth roadmap for managing their fee range. This calls for the capacity to manipulate one's spending and prioritize their fees, making the most in their profits.

Saving and Investing

Saving and making an investment is crucial for attaining financial fulfillment. With strength of will, people can set aside a issue of their earnings for savings and investments, building wealth through the years. This requires a protracted-term attitude and the capability to delay gratification, making sacrifices inside the gift for the sake of future economic safety.

Managing Debt

Managing debt is important for accomplishing financial fulfillment. With strength of will, people can keep away from taking up immoderate debt and broaden a plan for paying off any contemporary debt. This calls for the capability to govern one's spending and prioritize debt reimbursement, making development towards turning into debt-free.

Building and Maintaining Credit

Building and maintaining credit rating is important for engaging in financial fulfillment. With energy of will, individuals can extend a plan for building and preserving their credit rating rating, which can have a massive impact on their ability to get admission to loans, credit score rating rating gambling playing playing cards, and one-of-a-kind financial merchandise. This calls for a determination to accountable credit score score use and a willingness to avoid excessive debt.

Chapter 8: Health And Fitness

Health and health are crucial factors of one's existence, and strength of will performs a essential role in reaching physical and highbrow properly-being. In this bankruptcy, we are able to discover how self-control can help humans obtain fitness and fitness dreams.

Setting Realistic Goals

Setting practical desires is essential for achieving fitness and fitness goals. With strength of mind, individuals can set unique, measurable, feasible, relevant, and time-bound (SMART) goals that offer a clean roadmap for carrying out fulfillment. This calls for a excessive diploma of self-attention and the potential to control one's thoughts and emotions, which can be advanced via strength of mind.

Developing a Consistent Routine

Developing a constant recurring is crucial for carrying out health and health desires. With energy of will, humans can growth a recurring that consists of everyday workout, healthy ingesting, and appropriate sufficient sleep. This calls for the capability to prioritize one's health and discover time for healthful conduct, even in the face of busy schedules.

Staying Motivated

Staying stimulated is essential for attaining fitness and health dreams. With willpower, people can hold motivation via monitoring improvement, celebrating achievements, and trying to find guide from pals, own family, or professional networks. This requires a strength of will to at the least one's health and properly-being and a willingness to make investments time and strength in healthy conduct.

Avoiding Temptation

Avoiding temptation is important for engaging in fitness and health desires. With power of mind, humans can keep away from risky behavior and temptations, which incorporates junk meals or sedentary activities. This calls for the capability to govern one's impulses and make healthy picks, even within the face of temptation.

Seeking Professional Help

Seeking professional help is critical for accomplishing fitness and fitness dreams. With strength of mind, human beings can are searching for assist from professionals, alongside aspect personal running shoes or nutritionists, who can provide specialized facts and steerage. This calls for a commitment to one's health and a willingness to invest in one's nicely-being.

In give up, electricity of mind plays a crucial function in reaching health and health desires. By placing practical goals, developing a regular ordinary, staying endorsed, maintaining off temptation, and searching out expert help, human beings can accumulate physical and intellectual nicely-being and make a excessive nice impact in their lives. Through self-control, people can boom the capabilities and strategies needed to attain fitness and health desires, unlocking their whole capability and growing a pleasing effect within the worldwide.

Relationships

Relationships are an vital detail of 1's existence, and self-control plays a important characteristic in building and preserving wholesome relationships. In this financial ruin, we can find out how self-discipline can assist people gain success in their relationships.

Developing Empathy

Developing empathy is essential for building wholesome relationships. With strength of will, individuals can make bigger the functionality to recognize and percent the feelings of others, that might help build accept as proper with and rapport in relationships. This requires the capacity to control one's mind and feelings and a willingness to look matters from the attitude of others.

Communicating Effectively

Communicating correctly is important for building wholesome relationships. With electricity of will, human beings can enlarge the capabilities had to specific their thoughts and emotions in a clean and respectful manner, that would help construct know-how and connection in relationships. This requires the ability to govern one's emotions and reply gently and thoughtfully in hard conditions.

Setting Boundaries

Setting limitations is essential for maintaining healthy relationships. With power of mind, individuals can set clean boundaries that outline their limits and expectancies, that would help save you struggle and bring together appreciate in relationships. This requires the capability to prioritize one's needs and values and communicate them effectively to others.

Practicing Forgiveness

Practicing forgiveness is important for preserving healthy relationships. With electricity of will, people can increase the capacity to permit pass of grudges and resentments, that might assist assemble receive as true with and compassion in relationships. This calls for the capability to manipulate one's emotions and see the humanity in others, despite the fact that they make mistakes.

Chapter 9: Advice

Self-subject is an crucial issue of reaching fulfillment in all regions of lifestyles. While it is able to be hard to growth and preserve energy of thoughts, the blessings of doing so are big. By taking a proactive approach to power of mind, humans can acquire their goals, beautify their highbrow and emotional health, and make a extremely good effect inside the international.

As a very very last phrase of advice, right here are a few key takeaways to keep in mind as you increase your electricity of will:

Embrace a increase mind-set: Self-place isn't an inherent trait, but as an alternative a capability that may be advanced through the years. By embracing a boom thoughts-set and being open to getting to know, you may cultivate the electricity of will needed to benefit your desires.

Set sensible desires: When placing dreams, it is essential to set sensible, possible desires that align along with your values and priorities. This will assist you hold popularity and motivation as you parent in the direction of accomplishing your desires.

Develop a normal: Developing a ordinary that includes healthy behavior and prioritizes self-care is important for growing self-control. By making self-care a priority, you may increase the mental and emotional resilience had to achieve your desires.

Seek manual: Building a assist device of friends, circle of relatives, or expert networks will let you maintain motivation and live on the proper track as you determine within the route of accomplishing your dreams.

Practice self-compassion: Self-discipline isn't always approximately being first-class, but as an alternative about making development toward your desires. It is vital to exercise self-compassion and forgive your self while you make errors or revel in setbacks.

In end, strength of mind is a important element of achieving success in all regions of lifestyles. By growing a increase mindset, placing sensible desires, developing a normal, on the lookout for guide, and working towards self-compassion, human beings can domesticate the energy of will needed to gain their desires and make a extremely good impact within the global. Remember to be affected individual and persistent as you discern inside the route of developing strength of mind, and constantly be type to your self along the way.

Encouragement to Continue Practicing Self-Discipline

Developing power of thoughts is a difficult but worthwhile journey. As you continue to practice strength of will, it's miles critical to live inspired and endorsed to maintain your development. In this financial ruin, we are able to communicate a few encouragement and idea to hold practicing energy of mind.

Reflect to your improvement: Take a while to mirror to your progress due to the fact you started out training electricity of mind.

Celebrate your accomplishments and pay attention to the areas in which you've got were given visible development. This will provide you with the inducement and self belief to hold schooling electricity of will.

Remember your why: It can be clean to lose sight of why you started out out out training strength of thoughts in the first region. Take some time to take into account your why and the lengthy-time period blessings of strength of mind. This will assist you stay focused and induced as you continue to exercising strength of mind.

Find thought: Seek out assets of thought, collectively with books, podcasts, or motivational audio tool, with a view to will let you live caused and advocated to preserve training strength of will.

Practice self-care: Practicing self-care is critical for retaining the highbrow and emotional resilience needed to exercising strength of will. Make sure to prioritize rest, exercise, and wholesome eating to hold your physical and intellectual health.

Seek useful resource: Building a assist tool of pals, own family, or expert networks allow you to stay recommended and encouraged as you continue to exercise electricity of thoughts. Don't be afraid to reach out for assist at the same time as you need it.

In surrender, going for walks inside the direction of power of will is a hard however worthwhile adventure. By reflecting in your progress, remembering your why, locating concept, working in the direction of self-care, and seeking out help, you can retain to stay recommended and recommended to keep your development. Remember that self-control is a ability that may be developed through the years, and that the adventure is simply as crucial due to the fact the vacation spot. Keep pushing forward, live stimulated, and keep to unfastened up your complete potential with strength of will.

Worksheets and Exercises

Self-concern is a competencies that can be developed through exercising and staying power. To assist you growth and maintain power of will, this e-book includes lots of worksheets and carrying activities that will help you look at the strategies and techniques mentioned inside the ebook. In this chapter, we are capable to speak the worksheets and physical sports activities protected in this ebook.

Goal Setting Worksheet: This worksheet is designed that will help you set unique, measurable, possible, applicable, and time-sure (SMART) goals. It includes space so you can write down your goals, the stairs had to collect them, and a timeline for completing them.

Habits Tracker: This worksheet is designed that will help you tune your development in breaking awful conduct and forming right ones. It consists of space so as to listing your behavior and track your development over time.

Time Management Worksheet: This worksheet is designed that will help you control some time successfully. It consists of location so one can prioritize your responsibilities, time table some time, and check your development.

Procrastination Exercise: This exercise is designed to help you overcome procrastination. It consists of a chain of activates and questions to help you pick out out the underlying motives of your procrastination and boom techniques to conquer it.

Support System Exercise: This exercising is designed that will help you construct a guide gadget of pals, circle of relatives, or expert networks. It includes activates that will help you emerge as privy to those who can provide help and steerage as you figure within the course of your goals.

Self-Compassion Exercise: This exercise is designed that will help you workout self-compassion and forgive your self whilst you are making errors or enjoy setbacks. It includes activates that will help you reframe terrible self-talk and growth a more compassionate mindset.

By finishing the ones worksheets and bodily sports activities, you could observe the strategies and techniques noted in this e-book and amplify the power of will had to advantage your dreams. Remember to be affected character and chronic in your exercise of electricity of thoughts, and to are searching for manual and steerage at the same time as you need it. With exercising and determination, you may growth the self-discipline needed to benefit fulfillment in all regions of your existence.

Recommended Reading List

If you're interested in developing your self-discipline in addition, there are pretty a few books that could offer greater steerage and belief. In this financial ruin, we're able to offer a listing of advocated reading materials to complement the thoughts mentioned on this e-book.

"Atomic Habits" via James Clear: This e-book affords a complete manual to constructing well conduct and breaking terrible ones. Clear gives realistic strategies for habit formation, alongside aspect the importance of beginning small and specializing in incremental development.

"The Power of Habit" by Charles Duhigg: This ebook explores the generation within the again of addiction formation and affords realistic recommendations for converting conduct. Duhigg argues that the important detail to changing behavior is understanding the triggers and rewards that pressure them.

"Grit" through manner of Angela Duckworth: This e-book examines the idea of grit, or the combination of passion and perseverance that results in achievement. Duckworth argues that grit is a key element in reaching achievement and offers sensible techniques for cultivating it.

"The Miracle Morning" by means of Hal Elrod: This e-book gives a practical manual to developing a morning ordinary which could improve productiveness, strength, and commonplace nicely-being. Elrod argues that a consistent morning regular is critical for developing strength of thoughts and reaching success.

"The 5AM Club" thru Robin Sharma: This book explores the blessings of waking up early and gives realistic strategies for growing a morning normal. Sharma argues that waking up early can offer a competitive benefit and assist people gain their goals greater efficiently.

"Man's Search for Meaning" with the useful resource of Viktor Frankl: This book explores the human search for which means and purpose in existence. Frankl argues that having a easy enjoy of purpose is crucial for developing resilience and overcoming stressful situations.

"The War of Art" through manner of Steven Pressfield: This e-book explores the idea of resistance, or the inner boundaries that save you individuals from achieving their dreams. Pressfield argues that developing self-control and overcoming resistance is crucial for achieving present day and expert achievement.

By studying those books and others, you could advantage more insights and strategies for growing power of thoughts and achieving achievement in all regions of life. Remember to approach the ones books with an open mind and to encompass the mind that resonate with you into your workout of self-control.

Additional Resources

In addition to books, there are quite a few on-line assets and gear that assist you to growth energy of thoughts and benefit your dreams. In this financial wreck, we can offer a list of additional property and system to supplement the necessities mentioned in this e-book.

Apps and Software: There are a whole lot of apps and software program software tools to be had to help you manipulate some time, track your behavior, and stay prepared. Popular examples embody Trello, Habitica, and RescueTime.

Podcasts: There are many podcasts to be had that target energy of will, productiveness, and private development. Popular examples encompass "The Tim Ferriss Show," "The Tony Robbins Podcast," and "Happier with Gretchen Rubin."

Online Courses: There are hundreds of on line publications to be had as a way to permit you to boom electricity of will and acquire your dreams. Websites collectively with Coursera, edX, and Udemy offer a huge sort of publications on topics which includes time control, intention setting, and productiveness.

Coaches and Mentors: Working with a train or mentor can be a valuable manner to increase electricity of thoughts and acquire custom designed steerage and aid. Consider searching out a train or mentor in your vicinity of interest or in a related issue.

YouTube Channels: There are many YouTube channels committed to power of thoughts, productiveness, and private development. Popular examples embody "Thomas Frank," "Matt D'Avella," and "Pickup Limes."

By exploring the ones additional belongings, you may advantage greater insights and techniques for developing strength of thoughts and achieving success in all areas of lifestyles. Remember to method the ones assets with an open thoughts and to include the thoughts that resonate with you into your workout of power of will. With the right thoughts-set and gadget, you can gain your desires and loose up your complete functionality.

Chapter 10: Understanding The Role Of The Mind In Self-Discipline

I really have constantly struggled with electricity of mind and preserving a strong will. However, through my private enjoy, I actually have come to apprehend the crucial position of the thoughts in developing and keeping power of mind.

One of the key techniques wherein the mind performs a role in energy of thoughts is through motivation. When introduced approximately to accumulate a goal or assignment, it turns into an awful lot a whole lot much less complex to work out electricity of mind and observe thru on our commitments. On the opportunity hand, even as we lack motivation, it becomes a good buy more hard to push ourselves to take action.

Another way the thoughts plays a function in strength of mind is through our thoughts and beliefs approximately ourselves. If we receive as true with that we are capable of achieve our dreams and make splendid adjustments in our lives, it will become loads less difficult to exercising electricity of mind and keep a sturdy will.

However, if we've were given horrible mind and beliefs about ourselves, staying endorsed and centered on our desires turns into a good buy more difficult.

Developing a sturdy will and improving our electricity of will, it is vital to artwork on our motivation and mind, and ideals approximately ourselves. It may additionally comprise placing specific and potential dreams, finding belongings of motivation and help, and difficult bad thoughts and beliefs that keep us again.

One practical method that I in reality have discovered beneficial in developing power of mind is to create a every day everyday and stay with it. This facilitates construct momentum and set up suitable behavior, making staying stimulated and focused on my goals less complicated.

Understanding the function of the mind in power of will is high to growing and maintaining a sturdy will. By jogging on our motivation, thoughts, and beliefs and setting up well conduct and exercises, we are able to beautify our strength of will and acquire our dreams.

Another vital problem of developing self-control is coping with our emotions and controlling our impulses. This is in which the thoughts plays a important characteristic, as our mind and ideals can gasoline or hose down our emotional responses. For instance, assume we've awful mind about ourselves or our talents. In that case, it may cause emotions of frustration, disappointment, or even melancholy, that might undermine our power of thoughts and make it more hard to stay targeted and motivated. On the alternative hand, if we have got splendid mind and beliefs approximately ourselves and our competencies, it can help to beautify our self notion and resilience, that could help us maintain our electricity of thoughts and live the course.

One manner to increase more emotional manipulate and improve our strength of will is thru mindfulness practices inclusive of meditation or deep breathing. These strategies can assist us come to be extra privy to our thoughts and emotions and reply to them extra correctly and controlled way.

By studying to control our feelings and control our impulses, we are able to broaden extra power of mind and a stronger will.

Another important detail of growing electricity of mind is placing boundaries and sticking to them. This can incorporate setting limits on time and electricity and analyzing to mention no whilst crucial. For example, assume we're overextending or taking up too many duties. In that case, it is able to be useful to set barriers and prioritize the maximum crucial responsibilities in place of looking to do everything right now.

We can increase greater strength of mind and a stronger will with the useful aid of putting limitations and sticking to them.

Developing strength of will and a strong will calls for a aggregate of motivation, extremely good thoughts and beliefs, emotional manage, and putting barriers. By running on the ones key regions, we will beautify our power of mind and gain our dreams with greater ease and success.

In addition to the techniques already mentioned, there are some greater sensible guidelines that might help to improve electricity of mind and broaden a robust will:

Use obligation for your gain:

Having a person else preserve you chargeable for your moves may be a effective motivator. Consider locating an obligation associate or turning into a member of a help business enterprise in which you can percentage your desires and progress.

Take small steps:

Rather than seeking to overhaul your entire lifestyles in a unmarried skip, cognizance on making small, incremental adjustments that you may keep over time. This can help construct momentum and make staying inspired and heading within the right direction much less hard.

Celebrate your victories:

It's crucial to recognize and have an extremely good time your achievements, regardless of how small. This can help to boost your self warranty and motivation and make it much less complicated to stay centered to your dreams.

Make it a addiction:

The extra you workout power of will and make it a addiction, the less tough it will become. Start through setting small, workable goals and steadily constructing as plenty as larger demanding situations as you turn out to be greater cushty with the device.

Seek assist:

Don't be afraid to are looking for help or advice while you need it. Whether it's miles a depended on friend, a mentor, or a professional therapist,

having a person to reveal to can be a treasured supply of useful resource and motivation.

By enforcing the ones strategies and techniques, you could decorate your strength of will and growth a sturdy will to help you reap your dreams and live a extra fun life.

Chapter 11: Setting Clear, Realistic Goals For Motivation And Focus

Setting easy and realistic desires can be critical in developing motivation and interest.

When you vicinity clean dreams, you have got were given a clean enjoy of course and recognize what to do to gain them. It allow you to live recommended due to the fact you truely apprehend what you are working in the direction of and might see improvement as you pass closer to accomplishing your dreams.

Setting practical goals is also crucial because it lets in you stay centered on what is manageable. You may additionally emerge as frustrated or demotivated in case you set unrealistic goals due to the truth you can not reap them. On the opportunity hand, putting practical desires lets in you to recognition on what you could gain and facilitates you stay stimulated due to the truth you are more likely to succeed.

Prioritizing your dreams is likewise vital as it allows you recognition at the most critical obligations first and allows you manage some time greater effectively. By prioritizing your desires, you can make certain which you are making improvement at the matters which might be maximum vital to you and now not dropping time on responsibilities that are not as vital.

Setting and prioritizing clean and realistic goals can help increase motivation and interest via presenting a smooth direction and assisting you control it sluggish successfully.

As an expert, I can let you know that placing and prioritizing easy and sensible dreams is important to achievement in any area of lifestyles.

When you located clean goals, you have got a easy revel in of course and a roadmap for conducting them. This will allow you to live inspired because of the truth you genuinely understand what you are going for walks toward and can see progress as you pass inside the direction of attaining your desires.

It's vital to ensure that your dreams are sensible and plausible. You may also turn out to be annoyed or demotivated in case you set unrealistic dreams because of the reality you can not obtain them.

On the opposite hand, putting practical desires lets in you to interest on what you could gain and permits you stay encouraged because you're more likely to acquire fulfillment.

Prioritizing your desires is also key as it allows you reputation at the most crucial responsibilities first and permits you manipulate it slow extra successfully. By prioritizing your desires, you can ensure which you are making development at the subjects which is probably maximum important to you and not dropping time on obligations that are not as crucial.

Setting and prioritizing clean and realistic goals is vital to mission success and staying stimulated. By setting easy dreams, you've got had been given a clean sense of course and a roadmap for undertaking them. By making sure your desires are practical and possible, you may live caused and centered on what you could benefit. And with the useful resource of the usage of prioritizing your desires, you could make certain which you are progressing at the most essential responsibilities and coping with it gradual effectively.

Setting and prioritizing clean and sensible desires is key to a hit time control and achieving your dreams.

Here are some more guidelines for placing and prioritizing clean and realistic desires:

Be specific:

Make splendid that your desires are unique and genuinely described. This will help you understand exactly what to do to acquire them.

Make them measurable: Make positive your goals are measurable to music your progress and realize when you have carried out them.

Set final dates:

Give your self a cut-off date for reaching your desires to help you stay focused and stimulated.

Make them feasible:

Make sure your desires are realistic and feasible, given your contemporary belongings and constraints.

Please purpose them to relevant: Ensure your dreams are relevant on your common imaginative and prescient and priorities.

Prioritize your goals:

Make a listing of them and prioritize them based on their significance and urgency. This will help you cognizance at the maximum essential responsibilities first.

Review and alter your dreams:

Regularly evaluate and regulate your goals as had to ensure which you are making improvement and staying on the right track.

By following the ones suggestions, you could set and prioritize clean and realistic goals to help you live stimulated and centered on reaching success.

Chapter 12: Overcoming Procrastination And Building Good Habits

Procrastination is a not unusual hassle that influences humans of all ages and professions. It may be described as suspending or delaying responsibilities or sports that ought to be finished proper away.

Procrastination could have vital effects, together with not noted closing dates, decreased productivity, and reduced normal pride with one's artwork or private lifestyles.

In my private enjoy, overcoming procrastination has been a regular project. I regularly discover myself doing away with obligations I realize want to be performed, whether or not or not a chunk assignment or family chores. This regularly results in feelings of stress and guilt and a revel in of being beaten.

To overcome procrastination, I certainly have had to growth extremely good behavior that assist me live at the proper track.

One of these conduct is setting specific dreams and time limits for obligations. This permits me live focused and taken on and offers me a revel in of accomplishment as soon as I whole a mission.

I additionally attempt to interrupt large duties into smaller, greater viable chunks, making them feel a whole lot a lot much less overwhelming.

Another addiction that has helped me triumph over procrastination is putting aside devoted time for focused paintings. I try to put off distractions as a notable deal as possible by way of turning off my smartphone or finding a quiet place of job. This lets in me stay targeted and keep away from the temptation of getting rid of obligations.

I truely have determined that it's far important to be type to myself and not beat myself up after I do procrastinate. Instead, I attempt to emerge as aware about the underlying purpose of my procrastination and paintings to deal with it.

This ought to mean looking for greater help or belongings or permitting me to take a damage and recharge at the same time as favored.

Overcoming procrastination calls for discipline, self-recognition, and a willingness to strive new techniques. By growing correct conduct and being kind to ourselves, we can stay at the right tune and achieve our dreams.

Another technique that has helped me conquer procrastination is the use of a planner or to-do list. By writing down my duties and priorities, I can visualize my workload and prioritize my time. I additionally try and time table my most crucial or difficult obligations for the times of day as quickly as I am maximum inexperienced.

Another technique that has been beneficial for me is to set small rewards for myself as incentives to complete responsibilities. For example, I could probable watch a fave TV show or take a short stroll after finishing a mainly hard challenge. This allows to break up the paintings day and gives me a few trouble to look ahead to.

I actually have additionally determined it beneficial to enlist the aid of others in overcoming procrastination. This have to advocate looking for the assist of a mentor or train or truely sharing my desires and progress with a relied on buddy or family member. Having a person to hold me accountable may be a effective motivator and help me stay on route.

Ultimately, overcoming procrastination is a journey that requires ongoing strive and self-reflected picture. It is essential to be affected man or woman with ourselves and to understand that it's miles everyday to encounter setbacks and demanding situations alongside the way.

We can overcome procrastination and attain our desires through using developing right conduct and looking for manual whilst wanted.

In addition to the techniques referred to above, a few more strategies can assist conquer procrastination. One such approach is the "five-minute rule," in which you make a decision to operating on a challenge for five minutes. Once you begin, you could often find out that you may hold running for longer than 5 minutes.

Another method is to try to emerge as privy to the underlying reason of your procrastination.

For example, are you feeling crushed through the scope of the challenge? Do you lack the critical property or competencies to complete it? Understanding the inspiration purpose of your procrastination will can help you to expand strategies to address it.

It additionally may be useful to change your environment to make it greater conducive to productivity. This ought to endorse locating a quiet workspace or removing distractions which encompass social media or tv. By growing a more targeted environment, you could beautify your capability to pay attention and live on course.

Overcoming procrastination requires difficulty, self-attention, and a willingness to attempt new techniques. By setting specific desires and final dates, breaking responsibilities down into smaller chunks, placing aside devoted time for targeted art work, and on the lookout for assist whilst wanted, you may amplify super behavior that will help you live on direction and attain your desires.

Chapter 13: The Power Of Positive Thinking And Self-Discipline

The electricity of great questioning and the significance of thoughts-set in self-control can't be overstated.

In my very very own lifestyles, I certainly have visible firsthand how having a super outlook and cultivating a healthy highbrow mindset can reason advanced achievement and accomplishment.

When I even have turn out to be greater younger, I struggled with motivation and observed it tough to live on undertaking for even smooth duties.

However, my overall performance advanced appreciably as I targeted greater on growing exceptional conduct which encompass setting goals, visualizing outcomes, and putting forward myself with encouraging terms.

My self-control soared as fast as I observed the perception that I must advantage some thing if I placed enough try into it.

Nowadays, no matter what undertaking or trouble arises, I stay steadfast in my notion that I can overcome any impediment with tough art work and strength of mind. This thoughts-set has enabled me to live targeted at the maximum critical duties, allowing me to attain areas of my life that had been once taken into consideration unreachable.

The power of first-rate questioning is not a delusion. It is a very real and effective strain that may be harnessed to accumulate great consequences.

When you adopt an mind-set of positivity and reputation on growing your highbrow power and energy of mind, the sky may be the limit for what you could attain.

The key's never giving up on your self, regardless of how tough subjects may also moreover appear. Anything is doable with enough willpower and persistence!

By know-how the energy of terrific thinking and its importance in strength of mind, you could open your self as much as a global of opportunities.

So make an effort to domesticate your mental energy and trust in yourself - you can do some thing!

You need to be inclined to do the hard paintings and make it appear. With enough determination and strength of mind, fulfillment is yours for the taking!

The strength of great thinking and the importance of mind-set in energy of will is paramount.

By specializing in developing your intellectual strength, you will reap stages of achievement which have been as quick as taken into consideration improbable.

It may not be clean at the start, however with dedication and perseverance, you can free up your actual functionality and reach heights you in no manner concept feasible!

We've all heard the word "count on effective," but what does it advocate?

The "incredible wondering" movement commenced within the overdue 19th century to elevate the vanity of people who felt depressed, aggravating, or hopeless.

It have emerge as promoted on a large scale through way of way of Norman Vincent Peale, who, after suffering emotional issues himself, determined to assist others conquer their mental turmoil thru electricity of will and determination.

After his e-book "The Power of Positive Thinking" have emerge as a achievement in 1952, the writer inspired many others spherical him to strive first-rate questioning and benefit their goals.

In the 1960s and early Seventies, Hollywood movies started out recommending wonderful thinking as a remedy for despair. This became in particular established in movies that featured a male protagonist. By 1980, 90 three% of all U.S. Psychology university college students had been taught superb wondering strategies to therapy highbrow and emotional problems.

In the 1990s, self-help books have grow to be fairly famous inside the United States and made loads of heaps of bucks in income by way of using promoting fantastic mind and strength of mind to treatment troubles, boom self belief and attain fulfillment.

This have end up known as the "first-rate thinking movement."

In North America, "notable wondering" has end up synonymous with being positive, enthusiastic, or assured approximately one's existence and destiny achievements.

Promotes an unwavering perception within the inherent goodness of humankind and a conviction that "not whatever is impossible."

As the energy of great questioning have grow to be famous, motivational audio device started to seem on tv.

Many of cutting-edge outstanding-promoting authors commenced out their careers as life coaches and motivational audio system. In many techniques, they maintain to promote the genuine message that doing extra, believing more, and searching ahead more complete-heartedly can treatment problems. Positive questioning is now on anyone's lips with radio indicates, books, and seminars selling every emotional or bodily sickness feasible; "excessive remarkable questioning" is a treatment for everything from horrible breath to premature graying hair.

The "tremendous questioning" concept has been used to sell power of mind and beautify highbrow health.

While some people have used the method for its meant benefits, others have used it to govern or manipulate.

In modern-day instances, complaint has been leveled at using excessive satisfactory wondering, emphasizing the power of first-class questioning to overcome problems.

The power of effective thinking does no longer without a doubt rely upon removing horrific emotions and thoughts or cultivating a perception that the whole lot will turn out first-class if you are surely exceptional sufficient. It revolves around a completely deep information and facts of the human mind and the way humans way facts.

To recognize this, we want to test why notable thinking can negatively have an impact on some people. If you're recommended to "assume high-quality," there's no mechanism to maintain your thoughts from wandering. This manner there may be no manner of expertise in case you are without a doubt focused for your desires.

When the thoughts wanders off and also you lose cognizance, it cannot be clean to deliver your self lower returned heading inside the proper route.

This is why the energy of excellent questioning methodologies teaches us the manner to live targeted on what's crucial and brush aside the whole thing else as unimportant or pointless. In this manner, we're able to maintain our minds firmly focused on what matters maximum in our lives.

By doing this, we're able to keep away from distractions and distractions and preserve a smooth recognition on what's critical.

Our mind grow to be greater excessive fine at the same time as we try this because of the fact they may be focused on what's important to us.

Another issue with amazing questioning is that it may save you human beings from coming across their innate talents or the actual nature of their problems. When we anticipate all of the time truely, we end up complacent, lazy, and snug with our lives. We begin to enjoy that "everything may be awesome" if we suppose virtually enough. This is a trouble because it technique we do no longer take any initiative or movement to change or improve the state of affairs.

Remember, top notch questioning need to no longer be practiced pleasant for the sake of it. It have to be about identifying in that you are actually and then walking in the direction of growing the existence you need.

The key to advantageous wondering is figuring out what you want from lifestyles and then doing something to get it!

How are you capable of count on to expect sincerely about undertaking your desires in case you do not understand what you want from life?

The energy of fantastic thinking is a effective technique that might help human beings in plenty of methods. It is also essential to understand that it could also have terrible effects on a few people. To keep away from the pitfalls of immoderate excellent wondering, you want to first determine your dreams.

With a smooth facts of what you need from existence, you may be able to interest on your desires with determination and passion.

When it entails the electricity of excellent questioning, power of will is pinnacle!

The waft of best power, the chemical response, and endorphins created even as you suspect fantastic thoughts moreover prompt the reward center for your thoughts. This response is associated with specific addictive behaviors, consisting of eating junk food and smoking tobacco.

Positive thinking trains your mind to anticipate appropriate emotions at the same time as you devour or drink and at the same time as a few issue 'horrific' takes vicinity. That's why people with a strong superb mind-set can withstand annoying situations masses higher than people who are negative.

The subsequent time a person criticizes you or does a few aspect you do, maintain in mind to react with a pleasant mind-set – because it will pay off in the long term.

Becoming extra splendid calls for braveness and vicinity. It takes try to begin thinking clearly. This is a undertaking that many human beings shrink back from.

However, the benefits of exquisite wondering can also well outweigh the attempt required to end up super.

Developing first-rate thoughts calls for patience and exercise. You can also moreover furthermore need to position effort and time into growing your abilities to improve your questioning in reality. Just as you cannot be right at everything, you cannot assume truly in a single day. Keep in mind, even though, that there is no such issue as "accomplishing" effective mind. Instead, it's far a machine of superior concept and could.

Chapter 14: How To Overcome Setbacks And Obstacles To Stay Committed To Our Goals

I had normally dreamed of becoming a a success commercial agency owner. I had spent years reading and getting equipped for this career path and changed into determined to make it manifest.

However, when I sooner or later took the bounce and began my personal corporation, topics did no longer circulate as easily as I had hoped.

First, there were monetary setbacks. Despite cautiously planning and budgeting, I struggled to preserve the corporation afloat. I have become continuously dipping into my monetary financial savings to cowl fees, and it regarded like regardless of how tough I labored, I could not turn a earnings.

But I refused to permit those setbacks get me down.

Starting a business might in no way be smooth, and I have turn out to be determined to look it via. So, I worked even harder, seeking out recommendation from a fulfillment entrepreneurs and gaining knowledge of the entirety I may additionally want to about on foot a successful industrial business enterprise.

I additionally needed to face several non-public barriers along the way. I struggled with self-doubt and tension, continuously thinking my capability to make it in this kind of aggressive organization. But I reminded myself of my prolonged-time period goals and why I started this adventure in the first area.

Finally, after months of difficult artwork and perseverance, I commenced out to appearance some development. My commercial company commenced out to show a earnings, and I changed into capable of begin paying myself a income. It wasn't an in a unmarried day success, however I in the end overcame the setbacks and boundaries maintaining me lower back.

I determined that staying committed to my dreams required resilience and determination. It wasn't clean, however the experience of fulfillment I felt after I ultimately achieved my dreams made all of it genuinely nicely well worth it.

I faced extra stressful conditions and setbacks as I persevered to increase my enterprise. Sometimes I felt like giving up and throwing within the towel, but I knew I could not permit the ones setbacks defeat me.

I commenced to enlarge strategies for overcoming obstacles and staying committed to my dreams. I determined out to proactively are searching for solutions in choice to without a doubt reacting to issues as they arose. I additionally made a aware try to surround myself with supportive and top notch folks that believed in my vision and were willing to assist me attain it.

One of the most critical traumatic situations I faced modified proper into a lack of time and strength. As a agency owner, I juggled many awesome obligations and obligations.

It became smooth to get beaten and burnt out, however I observed to prioritize my time and set realistic desires.

I additionally determined the significance of self-care and taking breaks even as wanted. I set aside time for myself, whether or now not going for a run, spending time with loved ones, or definitely taking a few minutes to relax and recharge.

Despite those demanding conditions, I in no manner unnoticed my last purpose. I remained targeted and decided; in the end, my commercial enterprise started out out to thrive. I placed out that setbacks and limitations are a ordinary part of the adventure and that the crucial factor to fulfillment is to live committed and preserve pushing in advance, no matter what.

One of the most unstable moments in my adventure as a business enterprise owner modified into when I changed into confronted with financial insolvency.

I had poured all my monetary financial savings into my organization, and subjects have been not going nicely. I modified into suffering to pay my bills and maintain my industrial corporation afloat, and I knew that if I didn't discover a solution soon, I should need to claim financial ruin.

At the time, I had approximately $10,000 left in my monetary savings account, and I knew this could not be sufficient to keep my commercial enterprise for an entire lot longer. I faced the tough selection of each shutting down my industrial corporation and admitting defeat or taking a hazard and trying to reveal matters spherical.

Despite the priority and uncertainty that I have become feeling, I determined to take the danger. I contacted a commercial company train and commenced taking element to increase a way to preserve my agency. I moreover started seeking out new funding sources, whether or not or not via loans or investments.

It changed right into a frightening and unsure time, but I turned into decided to show subjects round. I knew that it would all be nicely really worth it if I might also moreover need to maintain on a touch longer and find out a manner to make my industrial agency profitable.

Eventually, my tough art work paid off. I emerge as able to regular a loan and make some key changes to my agency version, and inside some months, my commercial company enterprise employer have turn out to be decrease decrease back heading within the right direction.

It modified right into a close to call, but I had triumph over one of the most unstable moments in my adventure, and I became satisfied with myself for no longer giving up.

To overcome the financial insolvency of my business commercial enterprise organization, I needed to take drastic action. I knew that without a doubt persevering with to do subjects the equal way couldn't be enough, and I had to find out new techniques to show things round.

First, I reached out to a enterprise agency instruct for steering and help. They helped me to see the bigger picture and supplied precious insights and strategies for turning my employer round.

I also started out out searching out new assets of funding. I knew that I couldn't rely upon my financial savings all the time and needed to discover different strategies to finance my business organization. I done for loans, reached out to capability investors, or even considered crowd investment an choice.

In addition to on the lookout for financial guide, I made key changes to my commercial enterprise employer model. I reevaluated my pricing, advertising and marketing and marketing strategies, and product offerings to meet my clients' needs higher. I additionally worked on building a more potent team and relationships with key companions and carriers.

I made a conscious try to interest at the things that I must control. I knew I couldn't change the beyond or are looking forward to the future, however I can also need to paintings difficult and make the maximum of the winning.

By staying remarkable and focusing on what I can also want to do, I even have turn out to be capable of preserve moving in advance and ultimately conquer the monetary insolvency of my business enterprise.

During the tough time at the same time as my company confronted financial insolvency, I knew I needed to stay excessive first-rate and focused on turning subjects round. But it become clean to get stuck up within the worry and uncertainty of the state of affairs, and I decided myself stressful about topics past my manipulate.

To fight this, I made a aware try to cognizance on the matters that I may additionally need to govern. I found out that I couldn't change the past or are looking forward to the future, however I may additionally need to take motion within the present and make the maximum of the possibilities available.

One of the topics that I targeted on come to be my business organisation model. I reevaluated my pricing, advertising and marketing and marketing techniques, and product services to fulfill my clients' goals higher. I additionally worked on building a more potent team and relationships with key companions and suppliers.

I moreover made an attempt to prioritize my time and energy. I knew I couldn't do everything right now, so I focused at the most critical duties and permit pass of the rest.

This allowed me to stay centered and avoid getting crushed with the aid of the desires of my industrial business enterprise.

Several techniques will will will let you conquer setbacks and obstacles and live dedicated to your desires:

Reflect in your values and the reason at the back of your dreams:

Understanding your values and the motives within the back of your dreams can help you stay recommended and committed, even supposing faced with demanding situations.

Break your desires down into smaller, extra doable steps:

By breaking your goals down into smaller steps, you could make development generally and live encouraged.

Seek assist from others:

Surrounding your self with supportive people allow you to stay focused and recommended, especially while confronted with disturbing conditions.

Use exceptional self-communicate:

Positively talk to yourself and remind yourself of your strengths and abilities. This will allow you to live confident and motivated.

Practice gratitude:

Focusing on what you're grateful for assist you to stay effective and recommended, even when faced with setbacks.

Stay flexible and adaptable:

Be open to adjusting your desires or technique if wanted. This will allow you to stay devoted for your desires, although faced with surprising demanding conditions.

Find strategies to live stimulated and engaged:

Find sports activities or interests which you enjoy, and that help you stay inspired and engaged to your goals.

By adopting those strategies, you may triumph over setbacks and barriers and live committed for your dreams.

I made awesome to take care of myself and workout self-care. I knew I couldn't be at my fine if I have been burnt out or exhausted, so I made time for exercising, rest, and spending time with loved ones.

By focusing at the matters I may additionally need to govern and letting skip of the relaxation, I might also want to stay awesome and inspired, even during the maximum hard times. This helped me triumph over my business's monetary insolvency and ultimately achieve success.

Chapter 15: Building Self-Discipline With Self-Awareness And Mindfulness

Self-attention and mindfulness are essential additives within the gadget of constructing power of mind. Without self-attention, it isn't smooth to recognize one's motivations, behaviors, and conduct.

This can motive a lack of manage over the ones elements of 1's existence, resulting in a loss of strength of mind.

On the possibility hand, training mindfulness permits one to be present in the meantime and be privy to their mind, emotions, and actions. This heightened attention permits people to make greater intentional choices, primary to accelerated strength of will.

Additionally, self-focus and mindfulness permit human beings to apprehend and deal with any awful or self-sabotaging thoughts or behaviors hindering their capability to exert strength of mind.

By becoming greater attuned to the ones styles, humans can artwork to replace them with greater powerful and wholesome behavior.

Self-recognition and mindfulness are important in developing electricity of thoughts because of the truth they provide the foundation for self-law and the ability to make conscious, intentional choices. Without those equipment, achieving the quantity of electricity of will essential for self-discipline is tough.

Self-focus and mindfulness moreover play a function in keeping power of will over time.

By often working toward mindfulness and self-reflection, humans can constantly look at their improvement and pick out areas wherein they may need to strengthen their strength of thoughts.

This ongoing technique allows save you the erosion of strength of thoughts and lets in humans to maintain progressing in the direction of their desires.

Furthermore, self-attention and mindfulness can help human beings emerge as greater resilient and higher capable of address stressful situations or setbacks.

By being privy to their mind and emotions, people can higher manipulate their reactions and select out out responses that align with their values and desires.

This helps to keep energy of will, even in the face of hard times.

Overall, self-interest and mindfulness are essential components of constructing and maintaining electricity of mind. By turning into extra attuned to 1's thoughts, feelings, and actions, individuals could make extra intentional alternatives, ensuing in improved power of will and the ability to gain their goals.

In addition to the sensible advantages of self-interest and mindfulness, intellectual and emotional advantages also are won from the ones practices. Individuals can gain a deeper know-how of themselves and their motivations with the aid of the usage of way of cultivating self-focus, main to expanded self-recognition and self-compassion. This can assist lessen self-judgment and increase feelings of self esteem, enhancing motivation and pressure in the course of reaching goals.

Mindfulness can also reduce stress and growth emotions of properly-being. Individuals can allow pass of horrible thoughts and emotions with the useful resource of focusing at the triumphing moment, allowing them to revel in more at peace and on top of factors. This can assist to boom power of will, as humans can higher control their mind and feelings in place of being ruled through manner of them.

The importance of self-attention and mindfulness in constructing electricity of mind cannot be understated. These practices offer the muse for self-regulation and the ability to make conscious, intentional alternatives, essential to prolonged energy of thoughts and mission one's goals. They moreover provide intellectual and emotional blessings, which includes prolonged self-recognition, self-compassion, and well-being, that might similarly beautify motivation and force. By incorporating self-interest and mindfulness into each day lifestyles, humans can collect and hold electricity of will, primary to a greater attractive and a success life.

Individuals need to understand that running towards mindfulness does no longer constantly require yoga or looking for a quiet, solitary place to mirror. While the ones may be effective tactics for some people to cultivate mindfulness, there are various amazing strategies to exercising this potential.

For instance, mindfulness can be practiced on the equal time as accomplishing everyday sports at the aspect of eating, on foot, or maybe the usage of. Individuals can domesticate mindfulness in any putting with the resource of bringing one's entire interest to the prevailing second and the sensations and critiques happening at that second.

It is likewise vital to word that mindfulness does not require a particular amount of time or length. Even a few minutes of mindfulness exercising can absolutely have an impact on one's properly-being and power of thoughts.

Overall, the important thing to mindfulness is that specialize inside the present 2d in vicinity of being distracted with the useful resource of thoughts about the beyond or future.

By incorporating this purpose into every day life, people can workout mindfulness in a manner that is each reachable and sustainable.

Chapter 16: Exercise And Self-Discipline

Exercise and physical interest can play a good sized function in strengthening strength of will.

Self-field controls behavior, thoughts, and feelings to benefit a favored purpose or final consequences. It is a key element of fulfillment in masses of regions of lifestyles, collectively with paintings, college, and private relationships.

One way workout and bodily hobby can give a boost to power of will is with the resource of offering a normal and shape. When we decide to a everyday exercise recurring, we set a cause for ourselves and create a experience of subject in our every day lives. This can help us increase the addiction of energy of will and the functionality to paste to a plan even when it's far tough.

Another way in which workout and bodily interest can beautify strength of mind is with the aid of helping us to modify our emotions.

When we've were given interplay in physical interest, our our our our bodies release endorphins, chemical substances which could enhance our temper and reduce feelings of stress and anxiety.

This can assist us to govern our feelings higher and make selections primarily based mostly on motive in vicinity of impulse.

Exercise and physical hobby can also beautify cognitive function, in addition helping self-control. Studies have examined that normal exercising can decorate memory, interest, and hassle-fixing abilties. This can assist us to stay centered and influenced whilst working closer to a reason and to make higher picks whilst confronted with challenges or temptations.

Exercise and bodily hobby can play a important position in strengthening self-discipline via imparting a habitual, regulating feelings, and improving cognitive characteristic.

By incorporating everyday physical interest into our lives, we will growth the abilities and conduct needed to obtain our dreams and succeed in all regions of existence.

There are many techniques to contain workout and physical interest into your every day habitual to boost willpower.

Some alternatives might in all likelihood encompass the following:

Joining a gym or fitness class:

By committing to a fitness center club or health elegance, you are putting a intention for yourself and developing a experience of form and place in your recurring.

You can choose out an exercising you experience, weightlifting, aerobic, or a fixed fitness splendor, and make it a ordinary part of your week.

Going for a every day stroll or run:

Even some component as clean as a every day walk or run may be a superb manner to beautify your electricity of will.

By setting a intention for your self to get out and flow each day, you may increase the dependancy of energy of thoughts and the capability to paste to a plan although it's far tough.

Setting non-public health goals:

Another manner to bolster your strength of will via workout is to set private fitness desires for yourself. This might also encompass training for a marathon, lifting a positive weight, or enhancing your everyday health diploma. You can increase the dedication and perseverance had to achieve success with the useful resource of placing a purpose and running inside the path of it.

Incorporating physical interest into your workday:

If you have got were given a sedentary undertaking, it can be useful to find out strategies to contain bodily hobby into your workday. This should probable consist of taking a walk in the course of lunch breaks, the use of a standing table, or doing some stretching or yoga at some point of breaks.

By staying active sooner or later of the day, you could decorate your strength of will and normal well-being.

Remember, the critical problem to strengthening your electricity of will via workout is to find a type of bodily hobby you enjoy and make it a everyday a part of your habitual. By committing to regular exercising, you can boom the abilities and behavior had to gain your goals and reap all areas of life.

In addition to the physical advantages of workout and physical hobby, many intellectual and emotional blessings can help pork up power of will. For instance, workout and bodily hobby can:

Improve your temper: As said in advance, ordinary bodily hobby can release endorphins, improving your mood and decreasing emotions of stress and anxiety. This can assist enhance your ordinary intellectual well-being and make staying precipitated and targeted on your dreams much less hard.

Increase your self guarantee:

When making a decision to a everyday workout ordinary and be aware the consequences of your efforts, it could assist to increase yourself assurance and arrogance. This can make you enjoy more succesful and able to attaining your dreams, that could in addition resource your energy of will.

Help you manipulate stress:

Exercise and bodily hobby additionally can be a excellent manner to control strain and decrease feelings of overwhelm. By focusing to your physical properly-being, you can easy your thoughts and higher manage your emotions, that can help beautify your strength of will.

Promote higher sleep:

Regular workout also can improve sleep high-quality, similarly supporting power of thoughts. When nicely-rested, you are more likely to have the energy and consciousness needed to address your dreams and make proper selections.

Overall, the mental and emotional advantages of exercising and physical hobby can be certainly as important because of the reality the bodily blessings of strengthening electricity of will.

By incorporating normal physical pastime into your ordinary, you can beautify your intellectual nicely-being and higher manipulate your feelings, which will let you stay targeted and stimulated to your goals.

Chapter 17: The Power Of Accountability In Achieving Goals

I even have continuously been someone who devices goals for myself and works towards conducting them. However, I frequently struggled to live inspired and responsible to myself. I may also need to get sidetracked or procrastinate; earlier than I knew it, my goals were no longer a issue.

One day, I sought obligation and help in reaching my dreams. I reached out to a chum who became additionally operating in the path of comparable desires, and we decided to fulfill weekly to check in on our improvement and keep every distinct accountable.

This smooth act of obligation made all of the distinction in my capability to stay targeted and stimulated. Knowing that I had a person searching ahead to me to expose up and record on my development stored me on the right track and helped me live committed to my desires.

In addition to the responsibility issue, having a person to percent my struggles and successes with have end up moreover relatively beneficial. My buddy have turn out to be capable of provide encouragement and aid once I changed into feeling discouraged and vice versa. We were able to encourage each different and push every unique to hold going.

Overall, the electricity of obligation and having a supportive community of humans has been useful in assisting me benefit my dreams. It has given me the incentive and encouragement to stay at the proper tune and attain my goals. If you battle to stay endorsed and collect your desires, I particularly advise seeking out obligation and useful resource from others. It can make all the distinction.

If you're analyzing this, chances are you could relate to the battle of seeking to obtain your desires and staying recommended. It's now not constantly smooth to stay targeted and dedicated, specially even as life receives within the way or we encounter setbacks. That's in which the electricity of responsibility and useful resource is to be had in.

Have you ever had a person hold you chargeable for some detail? Maybe it modified into a teacher or mentor who checked in in your improvement or a friend who held you to a promise.

Whatever the situation, you probable located that having someone to record to or method to helps you live on course and acquire your dreams.

I apprehend this has sincerely been the case for me. I used to warfare with staying inspired and dedicated to my goals, but the entirety changed once I sought responsibility and assist.

I placed a pal strolling in the direction of comparable dreams, and we decided to meet weekly to check in on our development and preserve each precise accountable. This smooth act of obligation made all of the distinction in my functionality to stay focused and stimulated.

But duty is not the best critical aspect in attaining our desires. A supportive network of people who can provide encouragement and motivation should make a massive difference. When we've got got a person to proportion our struggles and successes with, it can offer us the rush we need to hold going.

So, in case you're feeling stuck or suffering to stay inspired in achieving your goals, bear in mind attempting to find duty and aid from others. It can be truly the thing you need to live heading inside the proper path and attain your desires. So, do not hesitate to obtain out and ask for assist. It is probably the crucial thing on your success.

I decided thru my enjoy with obligation and supported the importance of being unique in putting my goals. It's no longer sufficient to say that I want to shed kilos or get in form. I need a clean plan and specific steps to acquire those dreams.

Setting precise and measurable desires makes it less difficult for me to music my development and stay advocated.

Another important element of achieving my desires is finding obligation companions aligned with my values and desires. It's essential to surround myself with people who help my goals and are devoted to supporting me obtain them. This can be a pal, member of the family, train, or mentor.

In addition to finding responsibility companions, I've additionally decided it useful to installation systems and exercising workouts to assist me stay at the proper track. This can be setting aside unique weekly times to paintings on my dreams or developing each day to-do lists to stay prepared and focused.

Ultimately, the crucial detail to reaching our goals is to have a easy plan, surround ourselves with supportive and accountable human beings, and installation structures and sports activities to maintain us at the right tune. We can live encouraged and committed to sporting out our desires thru doing the ones items. So, in case you're feeling caught or unsure approximately reaching your dreams, try looking for duty and assist and word the way it let you gain your entire capability.

One of the maximum vital traumatic conditions I faced even as searching out responsibility and useful resource changed into finding the proper people to paintings with. I observed that it's miles critical to pick out responsibility companions who're devoted to supporting me accumulate my dreams and who've comparable values and desires. It's moreover vital to establish clean barriers and expectancies with my responsibility companions to keep each exceptional accountable with out inflicting vain strain or tension.

Another project I confronted become locating the right balance among duty and help. I decided that once in a while I wanted greater duty to stay on the proper song, even as other times I needed greater useful resource and encouragement to keep going. It's critical to don't forget of this stability and to talk with my obligation partners about my desires and the way we can fantastic assist each unique.

Despite those traumatic situations, I've observed that the energy of duty and help has been profitable in helping me acquire my goals. It's given me the motivation and encouragement to live centered and dedicated, and it's helped me overcome setbacks and limitations.

Chapter 18: The Importance Of Rest And Self-Care In Maintaining Self-Discipline

Self-field is the potential to govern one's movements and behaviors to gain a desired intention or outcome. It is an critical tremendous for success in masses of regions of life, and it requires a strong feel of strength of thoughts and a willpower to self-improvement.

However, retaining energy of will can be tough, in particular while confronted with distractions, temptations, or exceptional outdoor elements which can undermine one's motivation. That's why it is important to prioritize rest and self-care to hold self-control.

Rest and self-care are important due to the truth they allow human beings to top off their bodily and intellectual power, this is essential for sustained attention and self-control.

Without sufficient rest and self-care, preserving power of will and staying endorsed may be tough. For instance, if an character is sleep-deprived or careworn out, they will have a harder time resisting distractions or making top decisions. On the alternative hand, even as an person is nicely-rested and feels correct about themselves, they're much more likely to have the energy and motivation needed to live focused and attain their dreams.

There are many strategies to exercise self-care and prioritize rest, at the side of getting enough sleep, exercising often, eating a healthy diet plan, and taking breaks to loosen up and recharge. It's also essential to set boundaries and find out time for sports that deliver pleasure and fulfillment, which incorporates pastimes or spending time with cherished ones.

By prioritizing rest and self-care, people can hold the strength and motivation had to stay disciplined and acquire their dreams.

Here are a few more factors to remember:

Rest and self-care can assist lessen strain and beautify common properly-being. Stress can damage willpower, making it more hard to interest and make choices.

By practising self-care and taking time to rest and loosen up, human beings can reduce their stress levels and enhance their fashionable well-being. This, in turn, can make it much less hard to maintain willpower and live prompted.

Self-care also can assist improve self perception and vanity. When individuals cope with their physical and highbrow fitness, they'll experience better about themselves and additional assured of their competencies. This can help them experience more recommended and self-disciplined, as they are more likely to just accept as right with of their capability and enjoy able to attaining their desires.

Rest and self-care can enhance productivity. When humans are properly-rested and revel in right approximately themselves, they're more likely to be powerful and green. This can assist them make the most of their time and strength and allow them to stay focused and acquire their desires more speedy and correctly.

It is crucial to discover a stability between area and rest/self-care. While power of thoughts is critical, it is also important to understand the want for relaxation and self-care. Pushing oneself too tough without breaks can cause burnout and undermine motivation and field. It is vital to find out a balance a few of the 2 and to prioritize rest and self-care as favored.

Chapter 19: Fundamental Principles Of Self-Discipline

Do you want to shed kilos and not become each exceptional character who fails?

Instead of intending to be an entrepreneur, would possibly you pick out to reach organisation?

Do you need to come to be a global-elegance performer in choice to a mediocre professional?

It all starts collectively along with your company belief that your method can be a success and your dedication to the technique.

An extraordinary instance of the energy of determination is weight-reduction plan." Research has showed that 20% of overweight individuals are a success at extended-time period weight reduction whilst defined as dropping at the least 10% of initial frame weight and retaining the loss for at the least three hundred and sixty five days," however "a elegant perception that almost no one succeeds in lengthy-term safety of weight loss."

An example comes from the people of the National Weight Control Registry, who've out of place an average of seventy three kilos (33 kilograms) and maintained their weight loss for added than five years.

What is their mystery? Commitment.

These people said that they did an entire lot of physical interest, on commonplace for at the least one hour a day, ate a low-calorie diet, watched their weight, and ate the identical way on weekends and weekdays. Their diets did not have any magical homes.

The danger of prolonged-time period achievement is significantly progressed after those people have effectively maintained their weight reduction for two to 5 years. What makes achievement more likely over the following to five years? It's even as you begin to boom power of will over the long time with the beneficial useful resource of sticking on your plan every day.

I weighed greater than 30 kilos as soon as I changed into 21 years antique. I decided on a food regimen that made enjoy to me—a slow-carb food plan advanced thru Tim Ferriss—as soon as I in the long run located out I couldn't maintain in that way. I located it for numerous months. I had in no way tried dropping weight earlier than. I became properly-versed inside the tips and strictly adhered to them, which incorporates the obligatory cheat day at the give up of every week (which, no matter the truth that I took it significantly; You could now not consider how hundreds meals I ate on each cheat day at the equal time as retaining my weekly weight reduction.

I succeeded proper away, not like the bulk of first-time dieters. There end up no need for me to attempt ten specific diets. In approximately three months, I completed my intention. I in no way went once more to how

I have become earlier than. As with the humans in the take a look at, converting my behavior and sticking to them made it smooth to preserve a healthy weight.

Why did no longer I have to try a zillion precise diets before I out of place weight? Because I realized that sticking to a weight loss plan and believing in its efficacy have been extra essential than the weight-reduction plan itself (as extended because it wasn't a daft one-food weight-reduction plan).The diet plan isn't the maximum important aspect almost about losing weight.

The key's your capability to paste to a specific weight loss program and preserve it until you get the results you want. It have become additionally lucky that I had religion that my healthy dietweight-reduction plan may additionally artwork. I didn't need to attempt a superb healthy dietweight-reduction plan. I failed to have to transfer diets to benefit my purpose due to the fact I modified into positive. The conviction that my weight loss program have to gain success is an essential trouble to hold up here. If I wasn't positive of the give up reason, have to I actually have the scenario and backbone to maintain going? I'm skeptical. The excellent mixture is performed at the same time as notion and determination are combined. By expertise that it isn't always what you do, however alternatively whether or no longer you do it constantly and with unwavering belief until you reap your cause, this technique to diet can be applied to every different factor of lifestyles.

The same technique I used for writing, enterprise, sports, self-self belief, getting to know languages, and saving coins. Commitment, the most critical principle, have become an vital source of my willpower and my mystery to achievement. However, it is no longer continuously smooth to commit. In factor of reality, so as for us to accumulate our dreams, we often want to overcome doubt and demanding situations quite pretty various times. As a result, we want to learn how to cope with adversity, every extraordinary "A."

The first rate foe of self-discipline: Adversity

When things are going well, self-control is not critical. After all, if you're triumphing, what have to make you want to surrender? In the middle of their first exercising, few people give up food plan or exercising on the number one day. Discipline and resolution are handiest out of area even as situations become extra tough and you lose the initial pressure.

People who are capable of persevere in the face of adversity are higher organized to overcome their weaknesses and persevere even as they're tempted to give up. And how are you going to beautify your functionality to cope with trouble? You bring it into your lifestyles and grow to be buddies with it.

You may be higher capable of address poor situations while you end up extra comfortable with them. This e-book desires to train you behavior and physical video games to help you become mentally greater difficult and, as a end result, be capable of be successful even in tough conditions. Putting yourself in difficult conditions and persevering via them will decorate your willpower. Because overcoming demanding situations and undertaking goals regardless of them will train you a way to be a winner, you could moreover emerge as extra determined and inspired.

Exercise: This Easy Way to Get Motivated

There is a well-known proverb that dates back to Persian Sufi poets writing within the 11th century. They tell of a powerful king who asks clever men to make him a ring as a manner to make him sense higher at the same time as he's down. The smart guys deliver him a ring with the inscription "This too will pass."

In his address to the Wisconsin State Agricultural Society on September 30, 1859, in Milwaukee, Abraham Lincoln covered the tale. It is stated that an Eastern monarch as quickly as requested his realistic guys to provide you with a sentence for him that could be normally seen and ought to be actual and suitable constantly. They gave him those phrases: Additionally, this could pass away." How masses it communicates! How rebuking in a time of pride! How comforting in the midst of struggling.

Use this smooth trick to reorient your mindset whenever you stumble upon feelings of discouragement whilst trying any of the routines or carrying sports described in this ebook. Reminding yourself that everything in the long run passes is a effective trick to help you bear the discomfort, whether or not or now not or now not you are going via it voluntarily (via way of, as an instance, forcing yourself to awaken at six inside the morning) or due to unforeseeable activities. I frequently lease this technique to preserve my middle; regardless of the scenario, I remind myself that it is best brief and that the tide will in the end exchange. It sounds smooth, however it really works in case you try it.

How to Develop an Unwavering Faith in Your Ability to Achieve Success

Although you will in no way be absolutely first-rate that you can acquire your dreams because of the fact that doubt will constantly exist, in spite of the truth that it isn't expressed, you could take a few steps to growth yourself-self belief and concern. The trick is to imitate what special people have achieved to advantage the same goal.

You might not want to worry as a first-rate deal about the unknown if you stay with a attempted-and-actual approach. If loads or masses of people have accompanied a particular approach and done achievement, no longer whatever will save you you from doing the equal. Follow a diet plan with loads of real-life in advance than-and-after snap shots and testimonies in case you need to shed pounds.

Learn from a hit businessmen who have assisted hundreds of recent businessmen if you need to assemble a commercial organisation.

Learn a hard talent from someone who has a whole lot of experience education it (and, ideally, a whole lot of experience analyzing in substantial in order that she will be able to higher relate to your state of affairs).

Your self-doubt can be lessened by way of the information which you are studying from someone who has finished the identical intention as you do. After all, you may be following a proven path in place of just wandering aimlessly like a baby lost inside the woods. You might also have the important device vital to begin growing an iron-like treatment to preserve going regardless of the situations if you combine this belief with willpower and the right mind-set—"this too shall skip."

You will benefit ultimately from this e-book's ideas. The goal is to decorate your baseline self-discipline in area of definitely presenting you with a fleeting experience of electricity of thoughts because of the truth you overcame a small temptation. Let's move at once to greater specific sports and sports that you could implement for your life to increase your very own concern with these important keys in thoughts. Please preserve in mind that the motive of these wearing events is self-discovery, because of this assisting making a decision out what works for you and what may not with regards to growing power of will.

FUNDAMENTAL PRINCIPLES OF SELF-DISCIPLINE: QUICK RECAP

1. Commitment (sticking to a selected plan until you benefit your aim) and notion that your long-time period plan will be successful are the important keys to self-control.

2. When matters are going well, strength of will isn't always essential. You best emerge as tempted to surrender while plans fail. As a end result, you want to discover ways to deal

with troubles. This ebook makes a speciality of the idea that deliberately putting oneself in damaging times is the handiest manner to enhance one's capability to address them.

3. Remind yourself that "this too shall pass" on every occasion you enjoy like adversity is an excessive amount of to cope with. Every obstacle in lifestyles is best quick. If you hold telling yourself that subjects will get higher quickly, you could cope with extra than you trust you studied.

four. To make commitment less difficult, you want to have unwavering faith in your plan. Ideally, adhere to attempted-and-real steerage from a extraordinary man or woman with some of practical experience. Take, for example, a weight-reduction plan that has helped heaps of people lose weight. In the case of starting a corporation, observe a plan from a a fulfillment entrepreneur, preferably to your target employer. Follow an skilled teacher's motion plan at the same time as analyzing a new ability.

Chapter 20: Physical Excellence Leads To Mastery In Life

Professional athletes are the diverse great examples of self-control and backbone. When a median man or woman appears at an elite performer, like a international-beauty tennis player, his capabilities seem accessible and natural." He become born with it," she says at the quit. He end up furnished with it. Furthermore, she is a protracted way from the truth. The difficulty she sees is an event—winning. She does no longer see the masses of exercise hours. His sore body, countless hours spent education, misplaced suits, and the whole thing else that contributed to his achievement as a tennis player.

He emerge as in no manner born with the ones abilties, and nobody else is. It is the end result of an extended technique that took years or a few years, now not only some days or perhaps weeks. His physical advantages, collectively with fantastic hand-eye coordination, may also have contributed to some of his achievement. However, he may additionally in no way have grow to be a global-elegance tennis player if it were not for the each day strength of thoughts that helped him deliver out those strengths.

Working on your frame to decorate your tempo, power, or flexibility is a superb manner to get began out within the international of power of will improvement. Without dedication, extended-term planning, and determination, none of these goals can be finished.

About 34.Nine% of adults in the United States are overweight, in accordance to investigate executed for the Centers for Disease Control and Prevention. To placed it some other manner, it's miles secure to mention that a massive part of the Western worldwide has not had a bargain exposure to sports sports sports for a enough amount of time to domesticate strong conduct of strength of will and staying power. Because developing the ones tendencies consequences in everlasting life-style adjustments that are not favorable to weight troubles, they in all likelihood might not be obese.

In his e-book "The Power of Habit," Charles Duhigg describes normal bodily hobby as a "keystone dependancy" that might bring about the formation of some of greater useful conduct.

Reduced threat-taking, overeating, smoking, and alcohol intake also can give up quit end result from normal physical pastime. You can almost at once increase the ones useful side behavior by using the use of the usage of incorporating bodily hobby into your daily everyday.

Consequently, bodily excellence is a critical aspect of developing a disciplined way of existence. And no, I am not regarding becoming a worldwide-beauty athlete or having exceptional frame shape. A super deal of vicinity in lifestyles is built through way of manner of continuously running in your health and fitness in phrases of your talents and genetics and no longer evaluating your self to others.

Because you can't assemble a robust frame in some months, it's a awesome manner to enhance your strength of mind every day. You can not help but discover ways to understand the device at the same time as you preserve on with a certain routine for months or years and begin seeing consequences. The magic takes region whilst you shift your cognizance from sports to techniques in your lifestyles. Success necessitates specializing in the journey and the system of that adventure (method), in preference to the (occasion) vacation spot.

Habit: Follow a Workout Plan Consistently

Going to the health club or participating in some other fitness hobby on a regular foundation is a extremely good manner to look how disciplined you're. According to a meta-evaluation, forty six% of individuals who made health-related New Year's resolutions gave up with the aid of June.

The International Health, Racquet, and Sports Club Association's facts on gymnasium memberships show even worse numbers: sixty seven% of human beings who have one in no manner use it. People who do not use the health club in reality make extra cash than folks who do.

Let's bet how disciplined those humans are... Getting the great frame calls for 2 additives. Physical activity is the number one. The 2nd one, that's arguably more vast, is ingesting nicely. Daily field is wanted to preserve a healthy diet plan and have interaction in regular physical hobby.

You will develop a sturdy deliver of undertaking that you could use to achieve one of a kind lifestyles goals if you adhere to those exercises on a each day foundation.

Let's get started out out out with exercise. I won't provide you with an in depth plan to conform with because of the reality this isn't a e-book about health. There isn't always any character-duration-fits-all exercise plan, just like there is no man or woman-length-fits-all healthy dietweight-reduction plan. The best requirement is to include a monitoring device of some type on your weekly agenda and to stick to it. For instance, you can workout each day, irrespective of what, for an average of one hour. You might not be discouraged from exercise through the climate, laziness, or the weekend site traffic out of your friends.

I like weightlifting and different anaerobic physical video games that assist collect muscle and provide you with a more potent, better-searching frame (that is going for ladies and men, so women, do not worry approximately getting bulky).Anaerobic workout is brief, excessive-depth sports lasting up to two mins that increase muscles, pace, electricity, and power.

Some proper options right right here are:

☐ Sprinting in particular hill sprints, which can be extra stable for joints, greater effective for fat loss, and lots more annoying than normal sprints on flat terrain is probably the outstanding preference for nearly all of human beings because of its capacity to boom your whole frame in best concord. Contrary to a well-known photo, right weightlifting isn't always approximately building large biceps, however rather approximately constructing a sturdy frame with healthy proportions.

☐ Swimming while accomplished in brief, high-depth bursts as opposed to an hour-lengthy marathon.

☐ Yoga ca be a healthy manner for both males and females to get a well-rounded lean body. In and of itself, maintaining uncomfortable poses is a fantastic area-building exercising.

☐ Calisthenics or body weight physical sports can be a terrific possibility to weightlifting in case you always circulate as a good deal as more tough bodily sports.

The improvement of a properly-balanced, muscular, and wholesome body is supported thru using all of those sports activities sports.

In order to expand your problem, getting those outcomes is important. Your efforts to keep going irrespective of setbacks may be fueled via using development and reward, however preferably, the bulk of your motivation want to come returned from inside, no matter the results.

It is beneficial to include lots of cardio and anaerobic sports activities activities into your sporting activities similarly to anaerobic ones. The majority of the time, I do them now not for the fitness benefits, which might be obviously nonetheless essential, however as a substitute for the enjoyment and stress-relieving effects they provide (surely keep in thoughts that it takes at the least 10 weeks of ordinary workout to be aware vast adjustments in your pressure degrees). All of this has to do with field as properly. A character who's relaxed has an awful lot less hard time resisting temptations and sticking to his plan than a person who's overstressed.

The following are a few guidelines for stimulating aerobic physical video games that have remarkable health blessings:

☐ Cycling is a extremely good activity for growing power of will due to the truth extended rides may be mentally and bodily taxing.

☐ Walking or jogging is easy, less expensive, and gives you a runner's excessive.

☐ Tennis is probaly one of the most hard sports activities sports, or perhaps mastering the fundamentals takes a number of strength of thoughts.

☐ Inline skating is a a laugh activity that almost does now not enjoy like it's far exercise.

☐ When not finished ri brief bursts of excessive-intensity interest, swimming One of the exceptional kinds of workout for folks that are obese due to the truth swimming is less difficult on the joints than, say, on foot.

☐ Martial arts: the improvement of the mind is a top element of martial arts, making it a amazing holistic exercise.

How to Never Drop Your Fitness Program

The following are the five maximum commonplace motives why human beings drop their health applications and lose their power of thoughts:

The wrong type of power

There are sorts of pressure: every inside and outside inner motivation, moreover referred to as intrinsic motivation, is described as "acting without apparent out of doors rewards." We sincerely experience doing a little element or see it as a hazard to research, develop, and recognise our capability.

It is described as motivation that could come "from the out of doors, collectively with the inducement to win medals, obtain financial rewards, and attraction to interest from the media." External motivation is likewise referred to as extrinsic motivation. Because it consists of taking detail in sports activities sports for a reward that is outside to the approach of participation, that is called outside, or extrinsic, motivation.

Intrinsic motivation is the shape of motivation you need to paste on your health plan and beautify your strength of thoughts. You need to no longer go to the fitness center because of the truth you discovered a person will compliment or admire you for it, virtually as you shouldn't develop strength of mind completely for the cause of impressing someone. Reevaluate your motivation in case you workout often out of anticipation of a specific praise and find out little to no personal pleasure or leisure in the machine. When you keep doing some thing as it facilitates you achieve your full functionality in place of because it will make you look suitable or give you rewards, you enlarge strength of mind. Try a special, extra exciting exercise with a purpose to encourage you to find out, analyze, or realize your functionality if you cannot appear to find out intrinsic motivation. In the long time, you may not do it in case you despise it. In that regard, the second one reason is...

Lack of entertainment

Having quite a few location is high-quality, but that doesn't suggest you have to generally select out belongings you do not like. Don't confuse doing uncomfortable matters to increase with doing them.

A test on exercise adherence and intrinsic motivation grow to be carried out in 1997 via the usage of researchers at the University of Southern Utah and the University of Rochester. The people in a unmarried business organization went to Tae Kwon Do training, whilst the others went to aerobics instructions. Due to their emphasis on amusement, competence, and social interaction, the primary employer come to be greater observant than the second one. To located it each other way, they decided to take a health class they desired in place of one which modified into particularly designed to help them acquire their fitness desires.

If they weren't used to normal physical exercising, each alternatives may probably have made them revel in the identical manner, however they favored Tae Kwon Do, it definitely is the identical approach you need to take on every occasion you're making modifications that make you feel uncomfortable (like developing your workout or changing your weight loss program).Change your fitness plan if you do not locate it impossible to resist. Try to select at the least one cardio and anaerobic shape of exercise. There is not any rule that says you need to use this or that device even as you visit the gymnasium; there are numerous approaches to gather the identical dreams, even though the use of free weights in a honest way is commonly the best.

Even if I recommend doing cardio physical video games, you do not need to visit a gym class. Actually, I'm in opposition to it due to the fact I can't don't forget a extra dull manner to exercise than spending an hour in a room doing jumping jacks and other horrifying wearing sports from my PE instructions. Have a remarkable time moving. Join a pal for tennis, run collectively along side your dog, take a motorcycle experience and word what is round you. Go kayaking with a number of your buddies. It might be simpler on the manner to make it a everlasting a part of your existence if it does no longer experience like workout as masses.

Lack of help

Having enough energy of will to accomplish your dreams for your very very own merits praise. However, this does not recommend that it is the only technique. In point of fact, the guide of others can regularly both make or damage your resolutions.

According to a have a study, doing cardio sporting sports with a companion improves performance. A precise study indicates that human beings are greater chronic once they exercise with a slightly higher accomplice. It is because of the Kohler's impact, which states that jogging in a hard and fast calls for added attempt than operating on my own. When you work in a tough and rapid, you may paintings extra hard and broaden higher field, so why now not take gain of that and get assist?

False expectations

Regular physical interest teaches you commands approximately willpower: the way to examine a specific plan and expect the consequences with staying power. But in case you begin your exercise plan with the wrong expectations, you may probably give up in advance than you get more potent mentally.

You are in all likelihood to set unrealistic dreams and assume matters that can not occur in a particular time body because of the phenomenon of the false want syndrome, which incorporates making frequent tries at self-change at the same time as maintaining unrealistic expectations about the possibly speed, quantity, ease, and outcomes. Find out what form of consequences you may realistically anticipate and make the ones outcomes your desires to avoid discouragement. Small victories are more critical than aiming for the celebrities and not even touchdown at the Moon close to developing electricity of mind.

Lack of Time

A loss of time is usually the least convincing motive to wilderness a health application because it disguises a one-of-a-type form of problem. The hassle isn't a loss of time however as a substitute a lack of priorities in case you are unable to take care of your body. Although many humans's lives do no longer replicate the fact that fitness is the most important detail in existence, few could disagree.

In this instance, you could want area to decide your values and, most significantly, plan your life to reflect them. If health is certainly one of your maximum crucial priorities in existence—which it need to be because the whole lot else is incomprehensible in case you do not experience nicely—then you definitely ought to give up one in each of your a lot less vital priorities, like transferring up the agency ladder.

To provide you with an example from my non-public lifestyles, I virtually have some of restrictions at the forms of businesses I can run. For instance, I intentionally keep away from hiring entire-time personnel because of the reality they reason me an entire lot of pressure and characteristic a horrible effect on my health, at the same time as furthermore increasing my income functionality. My health is extra essential to me than material wealth, so I'm adequate with this tradeoff. After all, maximum entrepreneurs agree that having a team of complete-time employees permits you to gather a good buy greater. I need to possibly make extra cash breaking my regulations.

What kind of compromises do you have to make on your lifestyles, and do they align collectively together with your core beliefs? Do you prioritize your fitness and family over your career, however you put in 60 hours consistent with week at art work with out a clean method for reducing returned? Perhaps it's time to modify the ratio of tough paintings-to-family time. You have to have a much simpler time sticking for your exercise habitual and, as a stop end result, developing lasting strength of will if you avoid those 5 maximum commonplace reasons. However, preserve in thoughts that every of these troubles is supposed to help you emerge as extra difficult; it's far your responsibility to clear up them, not to apply them as justifications to surrender.

Side Project: Win Against Yourself

It is the first-class manner to boom strength of will to do some thing even on the same time as you do not experience like it. Working out way going to the gym and lifting weights or doing all of your immoderate-intensity sprinting and swimming ordinary at the same time as you do no longer experience discover it impossible to resist.

I remind myself that this is the maximum crucial day for me to workout each time I revel in tired, inclined, and normally unprepared for a exercising. That's at the same time as my area is without a doubt positioned to the test, and if I win, it receives stronger. You are already beforehand of the % if you may exercising irrespective of a slight bloodless (in case your symptoms and signs and symptoms are generally "on your head," exercise is remarkable), hangover, stylish horrible day, or a few different inclined excuse.

Like a muscle, those small victories assemble your clear up. You in all likelihood have enough strength of mind to gather anything you need in life if you can do it continuously for years. Now, I'll speak extra about this in a later bankruptcy, so do now not misunderstand and act contrary in your body. Don't be stupid if you've been having poor signs and symptoms and symptoms for days. Stop exercise and decide the cause (insufficient relaxation, excessive pressure, continual contamination, and so forth.) and are available again while you're organized.

Every 3 months, take in line with week-prolonged harm to keep away from burnout. According to a have a take a look at executed in Japan on training and detraining, even a wreck of three weeks isn't always sufficient to avert development on the fitness center. One organization of individuals within the have a look at changed into required to take three weeks off, on the identical time as the opportunity organization persisted to educate 3 instances constant with week. The first company resumed their schooling time desk at the begin of week nine. After 15 weeks, scientists measured the improvement of each businesses within the identical manner.

To placed it every different way, taking strategic breaks will not do any harm your outcomes and can offer you with a miles-desired damage that helps you mentally and bodily. Additionally, taking a damage after which returning to your everyday normal will check your self-control. It's a super manner to look how strong your fitness behavior are because it's extra hard to get decrease lower lower back to the fitness center after a break for humans with susceptible treatment. It is constant to expect which you have developed a sturdy dedication to exercise on a regular basis in case you enjoy restlessness throughout your week off and sit up for returning to the gym.

Habit: Maintaining a healthy Diet

It is one of the most hard factors of present day life for almost all of people. There are temptations everywhere: billboards advertising cheap fast meals, discounted costs to your preferred snacks at the store, pals inviting you out for a meal at a burger joint, or a quick pizza brought in much much less than half of-hour thru cell phone name.

Fortunately, weight problems does no longer growth truly. The handiest motive human beings are obese is their loss of strength of will, other than a few legitimate scientific situations (which do now not have an effect on greater than ninety nine percentage of human beings, so that you possibly can not use it as an excuse).If you want to come to be a self-disciplined person, you need to hold your weight under manage. This isn't an choice. If you can not deal with your weight, you could no longer achieve fulfillment in one of a kind areas of your existence, at the chance of sounding politically wrong.

In his video titled "three Things All Successful People Do," a existence train as quickly as stated, "If you do not find time for health, you may need to find time for contamination." When your body refuses to serve you, how disciplined are you able to be and the way a hit are you able to be? If you do now not care approximately your health, preserve in mind that it isn't always an "if," however rather a "at the identical time as." And this is not coming from someone who has constantly maintained a narrow determine. I appreciably applied to be obese and take full duty for my past. My private values and ideals approximately vitamins have been off, and I prioritized my amusement of food over my health.

In addition, I deliberately selected no longer to discover ways to change it. That would not imply, but, that I advocate following a strict diet of bland meals. You can although enjoy your food and be a satisfied, healthy person. For exquisite results, which weight loss plan want to you observe? There is not any correct reaction. The Mediterranean eating regimen, mixed/balanced (DASH) weight loss program, Paleolithic eating regimen, vegan food regimen, and elements of various diets had been all in comparison through Dr. David Katz of the Prevention Research Center at Yale University and a colleague from Yale. They did now not discover a winner, that is surprising (or no longer, counting on the manner you take a look at it).

As prolonged because of the fact the weight loss program became "of minimally processed ingredients close to nature, generally vegetation," it have emerge as considered to be useful to fitness and prevent sickness. Your frame will trade if you stay with eating commonly unprocessed meals. You can also even notice adjustments in different factors of your existence while these new conduct turn out to be a way of existence for you—no longer a food plan. You'll have greater electricity, which you can want to apply to do more bodily hobby that lets in you experience higher. You'll be able to examine new topics and growth as a person because you'll have extra intellectual readability. In addition, you could beautify your paintings ethic, in an effort to make it much less hard as a way to hold your new resolutions and achieve your goals.

How to Stick to Your Diet regardless of Uncontrollable Cravings

Switching from your vintage, lousy eating behavior in your new, extra healthy ones is the maximum hard a part of changing your food plan. Even if it has quality been a few hours because of the truth their closing meal, the majority of people in fact can not address the overpowering starvation or the choice to eat some thing terrible. Although certainly fending off whole food agencies is not the incredible approach (in the end, meals is a big part of existence's pleasure, so you have to now not deprive your self of it thru in no way consuming something a great deal less than a hundred% wholesome), it is critical to discover ways to address food cravings which will advantage more control over your frame.

When she is tempted to give up or pick out laziness over jogging on her goals, she may be much more likely to say no to robust cravings if she is in a characteristic to say no. In my ebook, the way to Build Self-Discipline, I offer more in-depth recommendation on the manner to deal with cravings: Defy the enticements and gain your lengthy-time period dreams. In the meantime, proper here are 3 smooth methods to cope with cravings higher:

www.ingramcontent.com/pod-product-compliance
Lightning Source LLC
Chambersburg PA
CBHW070118110526
44587CB00014BA/2014